THE SACRED POWER

THE SACRED POWER

A Seeker's Guide to Kundalini

Swami Kripananda

A SIDDHA YOGA PUBLICATION
PUBLISHED BY SYDA FOUNDATION

Published by SYDA Foundation
371 Brickman Rd., P.O. Box 600, South Fallsburg, NY 12779, USA

Acknowledgments

I wish to express my gratitude to Swami Shantananda, Dr. Deba Brata Sen Sharma, Stratford Sherman, Hemananda, and Anandi Siegrist for reviewing the manuscript and offering invaluable editorial assistance, to Professor John Grimes for checking the Sanskrit, to Ed Levy for his help in editing the text, to Eileen Considine for her skillful copyediting, to Cheryl Crawford for the cover and text design, to Angela Trinca for her paintings of the chakras, to Pat Donworth and Roger Wellington for checking and proofreading the text, to Stéphane Dehais for typesetting, to Judith Levi for compiling the index, and to Osnat Shurer, Sushila Traverse, and Karen Weber for overseeing the production of this book.

First edition 1995
Printed in the United States of America
02 01 00 99 98 97 5 4 3 2
Library of Congress Catalog Card Number 95-79046
ISBN 0-911307-39-7

CONTENTS

DEDICATION

This book is lovingly offered at the feet of Swami Muktananda and Swami Chidvilasananda, embodiments of the grace-bestowing power of the Supreme, who have kindled the flame of Kundalini in countless seekers and led them from darkness to light.

The Guru is the Supreme Cause,
the Guru is the ultimate destiny,
the Guru is transcendent wisdom,
the Guru is the supreme refuge,
the Guru is the farthest shore,
the Guru is the supreme wealth.
Because he teaches 'That,'
the Guru is most great.

— *Advaya Taraka Upaniṣad* 17-18

INTRODUCTION

India has a long and unbroken tradition of yogic discipline that dates back to the days of the Indus Valley Civilization or earlier. The large number of spiritual adepts who have lived in India have followed various modes of spiritual discipline (*sādhana*) as instructed by their Masters, and through their personal experiences they have enriched our knowledge of yoga. Information about the specific practices they followed is rarely available to us, however, as most of these adepts were reluctant to divulge the secrets of their *sādhana*. Yogic knowledge was largely transmitted orally from Master to disciple, and until modern times, that is the way the secrets of Kundalini were passed down to us.

For this reason, there are relatively few references and only sketchy descriptions of the practices of Kundalini Yoga in our ancient scriptures. Therefore, we welcome an authentic account of this particular kind of yoga based on scriptural references as well as the practical experiences of its practitioners. Swami Kripananda has done a great service in filling in the gap by producing this wonderful work in lucid language. It is based on the teachings of her Siddha Masters, Swami Muktananda and Swami Chidvilasananda, and she quotes liberally from the scriptural literature on the subject. It also includes many of her own and others' practical spiritual experiences.

There are different versions of Kundalini Yoga expounded by the various traditions, but the basic theory on which this particular form of spiritual discipline rests is the same. Its practice is not confined to India alone, but has been followed by a large number of spiritual adepts and mystics belonging to different faiths and traditions all over the world. Swami Kripananda has quoted from the writings of spiritual Masters, from both the East and the West, to show that this particular form of yoga cuts across the barriers of different countries and faiths. In India, Kundalini Yoga was practiced not only by the Hindus but also by the Jains and the Buddhists, who incorporated it into their spiritual discipline in a slightly modified form. This particular mode of *sādhana*, however, was made popular by the followers of *hatha yoga*, the *Nātha Yogins*, and the followers of the Shaiva and Shakta traditions.

Some of the ancient scriptures of India advocate that spiritual seekers follow a form of eightfold *(aṣṭāṅga)* yoga, including the control of the vital breath *(prāṇāyāma)* in order to achieve the awakening of the "serpent power" (Kundalini Shakti) and the subsequent piercing of the six *chakras*. The *Nātha Yogins* also stressed the necessity of regulating the movement of the vital breath, but they taught that the infusion of divine grace into the disciple by the spiritual teacher *(Guru)* played a vital role in the awakening of the divine Shakti lying latent in the seeker's body. The Advaita (nondualistic) Shaiva writers of Kashmir, who hold that the descent of divine grace is the starting point in the spiritual journey of the bound individual soul toward the Supreme, look upon Kundalini Yoga as the basic mode of *sādhana*. They consider it indispensable for the attainment of the ultimate goal, which is the realization of one's own nature as Shiva. References to this form of yoga are found in many texts, notably in the *Īśvarapratyabhijnam Kārikā* of the sage Utpaladeva, and in Abhinavagupta's great commentary on this work, the *Vimarśinī* (3:2:19-20). There is also valuable material in Abhinavagupta's own works, the *Tantrasāra* (Ah, V) and the *Tantrāloka* (Ah, V-VI), under the *Āṇavopaya* section on the *prāṇa*. The distinguishing feature of the Indian view of spiritual discipline is that it is based, as a rule, on the particular metaphysical theory of the school of thought that prescribes it; as a matter of fact, this provides the rationale for every step in the actual process of *sādhana*. This is also true of Kundalini Yoga, according to Advaita Shaivism of Kashmir.

Those who are familiar with the metaphysical thought of Advaita Shaivism of Kashmir know that the embodied bound soul, or *paśu,* is conceived as being of the nature of *chaitanya* (pure Consciousness). This pure Consciousness is not merely static self-effulgent Light (*prakāśa*); it is said to be of the nature of *vimarśa shakti*, dynamic illumination that always shines and reveals itself to itself, and is thus always self-aware. These two, *prakāśa* and *vimarśa*, remaining inseparably fused, constitute the integral nature of the Self. *Prakāśa* represents the static aspect of pure Consciousness called Shiva, and *vimarśa* symbolizes its innate, ever-vibrating dynamism, which is given the name of Shakti. Since every individual being is of the nature of pure Consciousness, both *prakāśa* and *vimarśa shakti* are present, even when the individual is in the embodied condition.

According to yogins, the *sahasrāra,* or thousand-petaled lotus at the crown of the head, is the seat of the *prakāśa* aspect of pure Consciousness, or Shiva, while the Shakti aspect of the Self is said to be located in the *mūlādhāra chakra* at the base of the spinal column, lying coiled like a serpent. The fundamental limitation that causes a person to imagine that he is imperfect is called the *anava mala*. When the spiritual seeker receives divine grace or *śaktipāt* from the spiritual Master, this *anava mala* that covers the Shakti in the *mūlādhāra chakra* is immediately destroyed.

As a consequence, the Shakti awakens and starts moving upward through the channel of the *suṣumnā nāḍī*, from the *mūlādhāra chakra* to the *sahasrāra*, to unite with the *prakāśa* aspect of pure Consciousness, or Shiva. As the divine Shakti begins rising through the *suṣumnā nāḍī*, the various *chakras* are revealed and illuminated by its radiance. The seeker is then able to see light of diverse colors and of varying brightness in the different *chakras*. The brightness of the illumination grows gradually with the absorption of the various elements located in the *chakras*, and it reaches its culmination when Shiva and Shakti unite at the highest level in the *sahasrāra*. This illumination is said to be brighter than the light of thousands of suns shining together, with the difference that it does not flicker or produce heat like physical light.

In some cases, spiritual aspirants are said to hear the *anāhata nāda*, or unstruck sound, which arises from the dissolution of all the *varṇas*, representing various aspects of Shakti, into the one primordial Sound, the *Paravak*. All of these experiences have been extolled in glowing terms by mystics.

The illumination mentioned above is sometimes called the "Fire of Consciousness" (*chidagni*), which, once kindled by the fire of grace from the spiritual Master during initiation *(dīkṣā)*, never dies. It continues to shine and illumine the seeker's intellect, and fills him with eternal peace and bliss. This linkage of the theory and practice of Kundalini Yoga has not been stated by the Shaiva writers of Kashmir, but is implicit in their writings. My own teacher, the late Mahamahopadhyaya Gopinath Kaviraj, shed light on this subject in his lectures on the philosophy of *sādhana*. He explained the significance of the term *chakra* (literally, "wheel") in the following way: As the Shakti enters a particular *chakra*, it whirls inside it with tremendous force. It gathers increasing force from its revolution and dissolves the elements into itself before rising up to the next *chakra*. This continues until the *sahasrāra* is reached.

This book on Kundalini Yoga by Swami Kripananda will be welcomed by those who seek to know more about the practical side of Kundalini Yoga as set forth by the practitioners of this form of yoga.

— *Dr. Deba Brata Sen Sharma*

Dr. Deba Brata Sen Sharma, M.A., Ph.D., is a retired Professor of Sanskrit at Kurukshetra University in India. An eminent scholar in the field of Kashmir Shaivism, he is the author of The Philosophy of Sadhana, *published by the State University of New York Press, a work primarily concerned with the Trika philosophy of Shaivism. He is currently translating into English Abhinavagupta's* Tantraloka. *He is a member of the faculty of the Gurudev Siddha Peeth Indological Research Center.*

AUTHOR'S NOTE

In 1976, at the end of his second world tour, Baba Muktananda gave me a beautiful and challenging command that has profoundly affected my life: he told me to specialize in the area of Kundalini and *śaktipāt,* to study the scriptures on the subject, and to spend every free minute of my time reading the *Ṣaṭ Chakra Nirūpaṇa, "An Investigation of the Six Chakras,"* a Sanskrit text composed in the sixteenth century by the great Master Purnananda Swami. In 1980, during his third world tour, Baba began to teach me some of the verses on Kundalini from the *Śiva Saṁhitā,* the *Praśna Upaniṣad,* and the sutras from Swami Vishnu Tirth's *Śaktipāt.*

Baba's teaching method was both traditional and mystical. He would drill the Sanskrit verses in much the same way a professor would go about it, checking the accuracy of the pronunciation and making sure the words had been memorized correctly. But Baba was also a great Siddha, that rarest of beings, who had merged with the Universal Consciousness and who consequently had access to the hearts of all. This invisible access allowed him to give me a direct inner experience of many of the verses he was teaching me on the outside. A Siddha is able to bring the scriptures to life; they never remain mere book knowledge, to be accepted on faith. Sometimes, with great wonder, I would sit for meditation and see the coiled Kundalini begin to glow with a fiery heat, like the burner on an electric stove, and then shoot upward through the *suṣumnā nāḍī* in the center of the spinal column. What I was reading about took on a reality that was alive and beautiful and gave profound meaning to life.

This book is an offering of gratitude for the immense grace that has fueled these years of study. It is intended primarily for practitioners of Siddha Yoga who have received *śaktipāt,* the transmission of spiritual power from the Guru to the disciple. The purpose of the book is to help these seekers understand their own experiences of awakened Kundalini and place them within a scriptural and cross-cultural context.

The first chapter gives an overview of Kundalini as it has manifested in different cultures and religious traditions since ancient times. The next two chapters describe the process of involution, the descent of the Supreme from its subtlest state as pure Consciousness down to the material realm of gross matter, finally assuming a dormant form in human beings, coiled at the base of the spine as the Kundalini Shakti. Chapter four deals with the awakening of Kundalini and the various methods by which the Guru gives *śaktipāt,* initiating the process of evolution, the path of return to pure Consciousness. Chapter five lists the nine different strengths of *śaktipāt,* from the most intense forms to the slowest and gentlest ones. Chapter six looks at the many different ways that the awakened Kundalini manifests in people's lives, within the four broad categories of *kriyāvati, varṇamayī, kalāvati,* and *vedhamayī.* Chapter seven depicts the *chakras*, their symbolism, the qualities associated with them, and the ways in which seekers may experience their piercing or opening as the awakened Kundalini Shakti rises through them. The last chapter describes the *sahasrāra*, the center of pure Consciousness at the crown of the head, and the final state of Self-realization or merging with the Divine, the ultimate goal of human life. May this work help to illumine the inner journey.

— *Swami Kripananda*
Gurudev Siddha Peeth
Ganeshpuri, India
October 5, 1994

Swami Kripananda holds degrees from the University of New Mexico, Stanford University, and the University of Madrid. Formerly a professor of Spanish at San Jose State University in California, she joined Baba Muktananda on his second and third world tours in the mid 1970s and, under his guidance and direction, began her study of Kundalini. In 1978 she took vows initiating her into the Saraswati order of monks, one of the first Western women to do so. Swami Kripananda's rendering into modern English of Jnaneshwar Maharaj's great commentary on the Bhagavad Gita *has been published by the State University of New York Press under the title* Jnaneshwar's Gita. *An engaging lecturer and teacher, she has taught Siddha Yoga Meditation throughout the world. She is a member of the faculty of the Gurudev Siddha Peeth Indological Research Center.*

INVOCATION

Just as in waving lights to the sun one is only offering his own light to him, just as in making an offering to the moon with the water of the moonstone one is only giving back what belongs to the moon, and just as in offering water to the ocean one is returning what belongs to it — similarly, O Source of all Wisdom, this work is addressed to You, composed of words that are already Yours.

— Shri Shankaracharya,
Saundarya Laharī 100

THE SACRED POWER

We pray to the Supreme Goddess united with Shiva, whose substance is the pure nectar of bliss, red like vermilion, the young flower of the hibiscus, and the sunset sky.

Having cleft Her way through the mass of sound issuing from the clashing and the dashing of the prāṇa in the midst of the suṣumnā, She rises to that brilliant energy that glitters with the luster of ten million lightning flashes.

May She, Kundalini, who quickly goes to and returns from Shiva, grant us the fruit of yoga!

When She is awakened, She is the wish-fulfilling cow of all things desired for those who worship Her.

— *Śāradā Tilaka Tantra* 35:70

CHAPTER 1

THE AGELESS WISDOM

Kundalini is the primal power of the universe. She is also the inner power that lifts a person from the darkness of ignorance to the blazing light of supreme wisdom, and grants one a permanent experience of one's own divine nature.

Almost all religious or spiritual traditions speak of Kundalini, the inner spiritual power, in one form or another. The Japanese call it *ki,* the Chinese *chi,* and in Christianity it is known as the Holy Spirit. In Mexico, Kundalini was once worshiped as the serpent-god Quetzalcoatl; the Kung people of the Kalahari desert call this same power *n/um.** Though the names used to describe it may be different, and though the symbols used to evoke it vary somewhat from culture to culture, Kundalini has been experienced in all places and at all times. It is clearly a universal phenomenon.

Traditionally, the knowledge of Kundalini has been a closely guarded secret, revealed by a Master to only a few close and select initiates. It tends to be spoken of only in veiled and symbolic language, if it is spoken of at all.

Once Swami Chidvilasananda paid a visit to Santa Fe, New Mexico, and met a number of Native American

*Pronounced with a glottal stop

women artists. They told her that they, too, know about the energy that is awakened at the base of the spine and rises to the crown of the head. In their tradition, however, it is regarded as so sacred that they are forbidden even to pronounce its name.

The poet-saints and mystics of all traditions have written and sung of classical Kundalini experiences, veiling the truth behind poetic metaphor. One such poet was Kabir, who wrote:

> Only a knower understands
> what our supreme home is like.
> Lightning flashes without any clouds.
> There is no sun, yet there is brilliant light.
> The pearl in that realm appears without a shell.
> There is no sound and yet the Word reverberates.
> All other forms of light are humbled by
> the Lord's effulgence.
> The Indestructible, Unfathomable lies beyond.
> Kabir says, That is my home,
> Which only disciples of the Guru can perceive.[1]

In the West, the knowledge of Kundalini has been transmitted by the esoteric or mystical branches of all of its great religious traditions. The knowledge of Kundalini is clearly present in the mystery religions of ancient Egypt, Greece, and Rome; in the teachings of both the Gnostic and the Neoplatonic traditions; in the Kabbalistic tradition of Judaism; and in the testaments of the great Christian mystics. In addition, various secret societies or "brotherhoods" — such as the Rosicrucians, the medieval alchemists, and the Freemasons—emerged to pass on the knowledge of Kundalini.

In Christianity, the Kundalini Shakti is called the Holy Spirit, and it is understood to be the power of God. The Holy Spirit is the creative energy in the universe and also in the human being.

A well-known prayer in the Catholic tradition — "Come, Holy Spirit, and fill the hearts of your faithful. Kindle in them the fire of your divine love" — sounds very much like the hymn we sing in Siddha Yoga, *Jyota se Jyota Jagāvo,* "Kindle My Heart's Flame With Thy Flame."

In the New Testament, the descent of the Holy Spirit occurs at Pentecost, when the Spirit is said to have rested on the heads of the disciples in the form of tongues of fire. Baptism in the Holy Spirit was originally intended to awaken Kundalini, and it is sometimes accomplished by the laying on of hands.

In *The Gnostic Gospels,* a rendering of an ancient Christian text, it says: "There is in everyone [a divine power] existing in a latent condition.... This is one power divided above and below, generating itself, making itself grow, seeking itself, finding itself, being mother of itself, father of itself, sister of itself, spouse of itself, daughter of itself, and son of itself...."[2] That infinite power exists in two modes, one actual, the other potential.

The Masons speak of the energy, or Spirit Fire, that rises through the spinal column. In Masonry, the science of human transformation consists of moving the Spirit Fire up through thirty-two degrees, or segments of the spinal column, whereupon it enters the skull.

The Hopi Indians of North America have always known about Kundalini. Along the spinal column of man, they teach, runs an axis, on which are a number of subtle vibratory centers.

The first of these lies at the top of the head. Here, when he was born, was the soft spot, the "open door" through which man received his life and communicated with his Creator. Just below it lies the second center, the organ that man learns to think with by himself, the organ called the brain. The third center lies in the throat, the fourth center is the heart, and the last of man's important centers is under his navel:

> The first people knew no sickness. Not until evil entered the world did persons get sick in the body or head. It was then that a medicine man, knowing how man was constructed, could tell what was wrong with a person by examining these centers. First, he laid his hands on them: the top of the head, above the eyes, the throat, the chest, the belly. The hands of the medicine man were seer instruments; they could feel the vibrations from each center and tell him in which life ran strongest or weakest.[3]

The Hopis believe that each human being is created in the image of God, but then the door at the top of the head closes and man falls from grace into the uninhibited expression of his own human will. Now he must begin the slow climb back upward through each of the higher centers, until finally the door at the crown of the head reopens, and he merges back into the wholeness of all creation.[4]

On another continent, a researcher named John Marshall led an expedition funded by Harvard University into the Kalahari Desert in Africa to study the Kung people. They produced several documentary films, the most interesting of which is *N/um Tchai: The Ceremonial Dance of the Kung Bushmen.* Marshall and his team discovered that the Kung dance for many hours to heat up the n/um so that the *kia* state (transcendence) can be attained, allowing them to participate in eternity. The n/um rises from the base of the spine to the skull where kia then occurs. There is a n/um master who puts n/um into the student and controls the process from then on. The Kung believe that n/um is not a physical substance. It is instead energy or power, a kind of supernatural potency. They describe their trance state by saying it feels as though they have a hole in their heads, perhaps two inches wide, which extends like an empty column down their spines.

The awakening of n/um also paves the way for physical healing. One of the Kung medicine men says:

> You dance, dance, dance, dance. N/um lifts you in your belly and lifts you in your back, and then you start to shiver. N/um makes you tremble; it's hot. When you get into trance, you see everything. You see what's troubling everybody. Rapid shallow breathing, that's what draws n/um up. Then n/um enters every part of your body, right to the tip of your feet and even your hair.
>
> N/um is put into the body through the backbone. It boils in my belly and boils up to my head. The thing comes up after a dance; then when I lay my hands on a sick person, the n/um in me will go into him and cure him.
>
> In your backbone you feel a pointed something, and it works its way up. The base of your spine is tingling, tingling, tingling; and then it makes your thoughts nothing in your head.[5]

Kundalini mystifies even the most eminent psychologists. In 1932, the great Swiss psychiatrist Carl Jung and his colleagues gave a seminar on Kundalini, and they observed that the rising of this force had rarely, if ever, been noted in the West. Jung said, "When you succeed in the awakening of Kundalini, so that she starts to move out of her mere potentiality, you necessarily start a world which is totally different from our world: it is a world of eternity."[6]

The Kabbala, the Jewish mystical tradition, also reflects a knowledge of Kundalini. According to this

... entire universe emanated from God in ten ...es, the *sephiroth,* each representing a cos- ...om the highest spirit to physical matter. ...aches that the microcosm, man, is iden- ...rocosm, the universe. So the ten *sephi-* ... within man and, like the *chakras,* are associated with subtle centers in man's body. The predicament of most human beings, according to Kabbala, is their identification with the lowest centers, with Consciousness trapped in matter. Through intense prayer, meditation, and the repetition of sacred syllables, however, the buried "sparks" of man's consciousness can be fanned into a blazing fire and liberated from their imprisonment in matter, in the darkness of ignorance. Man's consciousness can be raised from center to center until it rests in the *sephira* called *kether,* which means "crown," and is located at the crown of the head. When his consciousness rests in this center, the mystic attains an ecstatic vision of God and realizes his own divine nature.

The *sephiroth* emanating from God were often represented symbolically as a mystical tree, associated with the Tree of Life in the Garden of Eden. Interestingly, according to some Kabbalistic reinterpretations of the Garden of Eden story in the Old Testament Book of Genesis, the serpent is not evil, but is revered as man's greatest ally. It is the serpent who initiates man's search for knowledge of his own true nature, of his essential unity with God.

There are examples of the "serpent power" in the Old Testament. For instance, when the prophet Moses threw down his rod it became a serpent, and through its power he parted the Red Sea and found water in the desert.

In fact, the regenerative power of Kundalini has been

represented universally by the image of the serpent. Although in the West the serpent has come to stand for man's sinfulness, the mystic traditions take another view. According to the mythologist Joseph Campbell, the usual association of the serpent "is not with corruption, but with physical and spiritual health. It is symbolic of the power that casts off death to be resurrected."[7]

The modern French novelist and dramatist Romain Rolland once wrote, "I have rediscovered the key to the lost staircase — the staircase in the wall that spirals like the coils of a serpent, that winds from the subterranean depths of the ego, up to the high terraces crowned by the stars."[8]

Saint Ignatius of Loyola, the sixteenth-century mystic, wrote in his *Autobiography* that there was a period when he would often see something very beautiful in the air near him, which gave him great consolation. It appeared to be shaped like a serpent and was shining with light. That vision lasted for many days, and soon afterward he began to experience great changes in his soul, and knew that he was embarking on a new life.

The Aztecs of ancient Mexico worshiped the Plumed Serpent, Quetzalcoatl, known to the Mayas as Kukulkan. This feathered serpent-deity was regarded as the divine force of transformation and regeneration.

On the original altar of the Church of Saint Ambrose in Milan, dating from the fourth century, is a stone carving of a serpent coiled three and a half times —the same form in which we find the sleeping Kundalini in the Indian tradition.

And among the Australian aborigines, "the medicine man receives his power from a rainbow serpent or a water snake which can be seen in the sky. It is this snake that makes the man a medicine man...."[9]

> The medicine man is trained to receive and to use that awesome power that governs time, space, matter, and death. He receives it from the group heroes, the historic source of the group, in the eternal dreamtime, through an unbroken channel, a long line of medicine men....[10]
>
> Certain persons (abstracting themselves from what was happening around them and concentrating on the psychic power within them), practiced something akin to meditation... During such periods of meditation and vision, when this power and their own thoughts were as one, they would see visions unconnected with earthly life. They would go to the world of ancestral beings. This power is said to be present in all persons, but to be especially developed by a few....[11]

This power and the rainbow serpent are located in the human body in a psychic center below the navel. The medicine man acquires supernormal powers:

> He learns to see and understand hidden things. He will be able to see before his inner eye past and future events and happenings in other worlds. He learns to read other people's thoughts and recognize their secret worries, and to cure illnesses....[12]

Among the Tibetan Buddhists, many seekers of enlightenment practice Tummo, the yoga of psychic heat. When practicing Tummo, the yogi must meditate intensely on the *suṣumnā nāḍī,* the central pathway of Kundalini, and on the *īḍā* and *piṅgalā nāḍīs,* the subtle channels on either side of the *suṣumnā*, by using complex visualization techniques.

The yogi prays to his lineage of Gurus to confer their "gift-waves" (grace or Shakti) upon him. He prays to the Gurus, saying, "Grant your gift-waves that the vital force may enter into the *suṣumnā*. Grant your gift-waves that the ecstatic warmth of the psychic heat may blaze up. Grant your gift-waves that the impure, illusory body may be transmuted. Grant your gift-waves that Buddhahood may be attained in this very lifetime."[13] Little by little, the yogi acquires the power of enduring the most extreme cold, clad only in a single cotton cloth, or without clothing altogether.

In the tradition of Tummo, the Guru frequently tests his disciples to see how much progress they have made. On a frosty winter night with a hard wind blowing, the neophytes are led to the shore of a river or lake. They sit on the ground, cross-legged and naked. A hole is made in the ice, and sheets are dipped in the icy water. Each man wraps himself in one of them and must dry it on his body. As soon as the sheet has become dry, it is again dipped in the water and placed on the novice's body to be dried as before. This goes on until daybreak. The one who has dried the most sheets is the winner of the competition. The yogi is required to dry at least three wet sheets in order to be judged proficient in Tummo.[14]

Saint Teresa of Avila, the great Christian mystic of sixteenth-century Spain, describes her exploration of the seven inner mansions of the soul, and tells how, in the seventh mansion, the soul finally reaches the spiritual marriage with God. She says:

> In the seventh mansion is the King of Glory, in the greatest splendor, illuminating and beautifying all the others. Here at last, the soul reaches the spiritual marriage with God. It is like rain falling from the heavens into a river; it is impossible to divide or separate the water belonging to the river from the water which fell from the heavens. Or it is as if a tiny stream enters the sea, from which it will find no way of separating itself. This is the mansion which the Lord reserves as His own and which you will never leave.[15]

Saint Teresa also says that the soul is transformed by an inner fire that consumes all the soul's faults and miseries and makes it pure. She also describes her many Kundalini experiences, such as inner sounds:

> My head sounds just as if it were full of brimming rivers, and then as if all the water in those rivers came suddenly rushing downward; and a host of little birds seem to be whistling, not in the ears, but in the upper part of the head, where the higher part of the soul is said to be. I have held this view for a long time, for the spirit seems to move upward with great velocity.[16]

She also describes the divine inner light, saying:

> So different from any earthly light is the brightness and light now revealed to the eyes that by comparison with it the brightness of our sun seems quite dim, and we should never want to open our eyes again to see it.[17]

Among the Iglulik Eskimos, a series of initiations culminates with the "lightening" or "illumination," after which the shaman sees inside his head a luminous fire, which enables him to penetrate the darkness even with his eyes closed, and to perceive things and coming events of which others are unaware.

The Egyptian mystery schools also taught about the incarnation of the divine principle of light. First, this light descends into darkness, and then for the reascent enters the vertebral column of a serpent, whose name is Divine Life. It enters the serpent's tail and exits through its mouth, a journey representing the triumph of light over darkness and the transformation of the human being from the densest matter into light.

This transformation from matter, or darkness, to light and spirit, is the task of Kundalini, the divine conscious power that resides within us. This is why it is essential to awaken Her.

"When one acquires the strength of Kundalini," Baba Muktananda said, "one expands infinitely, and then one assimilates this whole universe. One is able to see the whole universe within one's own Self. One no longer remains a limited, bound creature. One achieves total union with God."[18]

Notes to Chapter 1

1 Many of Kabir's poems (see Glossary) describe classical Kundalini experiences. This poem was rendered from a translation of the original.

2 Elaine Pagels, *The Gnostic Gospels* (New York: Random House, 1979), p. 51.

3 Frank Waters, *The Book of the Hopi* (Harmonsworth, Middlesex: Penguin Books, 1977), pp. 11-13.

4 Ibid., p. 33.

5 John Marshall, *N/um Tchai: The Ceremonial Dance of the !Kung Bushmen, A Study Guide* (Somerville, Massachusetts: Documentary Educational Resources, Inc., 1957), pp. 3, 19.

6 C. G. Jung, *Psychological Commentary on Kundalini* (Zurich: Spring Publications, 1975), p.18.

7 Joseph Campbell, *The Mythic Image* (Princeton: Princeton University Press, 1974), p. 286.

8 Joseph Head and S. L. Cranston, editors, *Reincarnation, The Phoenix Fire Mystery* (New York: Crown Publishers, 1977), p. 366.

9 A.P. Elkin, *Aboriginal Men of High Degree* (Queensland: University of Queensland Press, 1977), p. 21.

10 Ibid., p. 32.

11 Ibid., p. 57.

12 Ibid., p. 143.

13 W. Y. Evans-Wentz, *Tibetan Yoga and Secret Doctrines* (London: Oxford University Press, 1958), pp. 182-83.

14 Alexandra David-Neel, *Magic and Mystery in Tibet* (London: John Lane, 1931), pp. 227-29.

15 Saint Teresa of Avila, *The Interior Castle,* translated and edited by E. Allison Peers (Garden City, New York: Image Books, 1961), p. 214.

16 Ibid., p. 77.

17 *The Life of Teresa of Jesus,* translated and edited by E. Allison Peers (Garden City, New York: Image Books, 1960), p. 260.

18 Swami Muktananda, *Kundalini, The Secret of Life,* 2d edition (New York: SYDA Foundation, 1979), p. 8.

Shiva can create only when He is united with Shakti. Without Shakti, He cannot stir. For this reason, how can an ordinary person bow down to You to praise You, O Mother, who is worshiped by the deities of creation, preservation, and destruction?

—Shri Shankaracharya, *Ānanda Laharī* 1

CHAPTER 2

SHIVA AND SHAKTI:

The Primal Parents of the Universe

Although the mysterious force of Kundalini is known throughout the world, the Indian tradition has structured and organized this knowledge into its most comprehensive form. Kundalini is worshiped in India and in many other cultures as a manifestation of the divine cosmic power that has created the universe, also known as the Great Goddess, the *Devī*, or Shakti. She is the creative energy of Shiva, the formless Absolute, and She manifests the universe out of Herself and within Herself. She has vibrated into all the billions of forms that we see around us.

Baba Muktananda said: "She doesn't create this universe the way a human being builds a house, using different kinds of materials and remaining different from those materials. She creates the universe out of Her own being, and it is She Herself who becomes this universe.... She is that supreme energy which moves and animates all creatures, from the elephant to the tiniest ant."[1]

The *Devī* is the Mother aspect of the Supreme. She is the creator and nourisher of the world and is worshiped primarily because of Her compassionate heart.

It is said that when the great sage Shankaracharya was living in Benares in the eighth century, he would go every day to the banks of the Ganges, where he would teach his students Advaita Vedanta, the philosophy of nondualism. One day he found a dead body blocking his path, and a young widow keeping vigil over it.

Shankaracharya's disciples asked the widow to make way for their great teacher, but she ignored them. Then Shankaracharya himself gently asked her please to move the body and allow them to pass. When she ignored him, too, he asked her a second time. The young widow looked at Shankaracharya and said, "Why don't you ask him to move?" This puzzled the sage, so the woman continued, "You teach nondualism, but you yourself are guilty of dualism. You have taught only half of the truth. You worship only Lord Shiva; you have ignored Shakti, the great Goddess. She is the Power that has created the entire universe. If you worship Her, you will be able to bring this body back to life."

According to legend, this young widow was the Divine Mother, who had assumed that particular form to teach the eminent sage a lesson. From that day on, Shankaracharya became a great devotee of the Goddess and composed many beautiful hymns in Her praise. In one of them, he says:

> O Mother! You have many worthy sons on earth,
> But I, Your son, am of no worth.
> Yet You should never abandon me;
> A bad son may at times be born,
> But a bad mother there can never be.
> I have no desire for liberation,
> Neither for wealth,
> Nor for knowledge.
> O Moon-faced One! I do not wish for happiness.
> I only beg this of You,
> That I may spend my life in the recitation of Your names:
> *Mriḍānī, Rudrāṇī, Śiva, Śive, Bhavānī.*[2]

Shakti has three forms or degrees of subtlety. The first is Her supreme form, which is unknowable. Next there is Her subtle form, which consists of sound or mantra, through which all forms vibrate into existence. But the mind cannot easily grasp the subtlety of these first two forms; so Shakti appears in Her third form, which is gross or physical, as a beautiful woman with hands and feet and so on, as celebrated in the *Devīstotra*, the hymns to the *Devī* in the Puranas and the Tantras. It is in this form that She is worshiped by Her devotees, who contemplate Her indescribable beauty: "O Bhavani! I worship Your form upon which Shiva gazes with great love, and who, as if not satiated by looking at You with two eyes, has made for Himself yet a third."[3]

The Shaivite scriptures describe Her as "the will power of God, the ever-young maiden called Uma."[4] She is ever-young because She is always playing; and Her play is nothing less than the creation, sustenance, and dissolution of the world.

Shiva is pure Consciousness, the static center of all things, the substratum of all change. The Shiva principle can never be seen; it can only be known by its effects. It is dependent on Shakti, the active or dynamic aspect of Consciousness, to bring it into manifestation. We can come to know Shiva only through Shakti. Jnaneshwar Maharaj expresses this very poetically:

> Now I pay my respects to the God and Goddess who are the limitless primal parents of the universe.
>
> The lover himself, out of boundless love, becomes the beloved, and the beloved becomes the lover.
>
> Each taking the place of the other, they reside on the same charming spot. They are made of the same substance and share the same food.

> They are so averse to separation that not even their child, the universe, can disturb their union.
>
> Seated on the same ground, wearing the same garment of light, they dwell together in eternal bliss.
>
> How sweet and mysterious is their union! Though the whole universe is too small to contain them, they dwell together happily in the tiniest particle.
>
> Each regards his spouse as his very life, and neither creates so much as a blade of grass without the other.
>
> Abashed at the nakedness of Her formless husband, She weaves the universe of names and forms from Her very being, and clothes Him in it as a resplendent garment."[5]

The *Devī* is also *Mahāmāyā*, the great *māyā*, the enchantress of the universal dream, the world-bewilderer. When Kundalini lies asleep at the base of the spine, the Divine Mother takes this form of the great illusion — the illusion of separateness from God and from the world, the illusion of duality and multiplicity.

To understand *māyā*, take a look around you. See what the world looks like: sometimes enchanting and beautiful, at other times frightening, unpredictable, and confusing; a world of myriad names and forms, of infinite variety; a world that even according to modern physics is not what it seems to be. The apparent solidity of the objects around us, the scientists say, is an illusion. The world-appearance that we regard as reality is actually vibrating energy, Shakti, the Divine Mother, "whose eyes, playing like fish in the beautiful waters of Her divine face, open and shut with the appearance and disappearance of countless worlds, now illuminated by Her light, now wrapped in Her terrible darkness."[6]

This cosmic Shakti also takes the forms of many individual goddesses, who represent the various aspects of the one universal Energy. In the Indian tradition Her three principal forms are Kali, Lakshmi, and Saraswati. Although their attributes and manifestations are diverse, each has the capacity to take us back to the primordial One.

Kali, often represented as the consort of Lord Shiva, embodies His power to dissolve, destroy, and devour. Dark and terrifying, She is portrayed wearing a garland of skulls around Her neck and dancing in cremation grounds. Yet by Her very ferocity She bestows the supreme boon of liberation, destroying our faults and weaknesses, our ignorance and our desires.

Many years ago when I was browsing through a London art museum, one work in particular captured my attention. It was a statue of the Goddess mounted on a lion, brandishing weapons in Her many hands, riding toward a hideous monster who stood at the head of his demonic hordes, armed and ready for battle. She was obviously about to take them all on singlehandedly. Part of me dismissed this image. What fairy tale does this illustrate, I wondered. Yet on some deep level it was extraordinarily compelling.

Years later I came to understand that that Goddess was Kundalini Shakti in Her aspect as Durga or Kali. When She is awakened within us, She goes to battle against the inner demons: desire, anger, greed, pride, delusion, jealousy, doubt, resistance, laziness, and so on. Despite the ups and downs we may experience in the course of our spiritual practice, She is ultimately victorious. She is the divine force of transformation that brings us from a spiritually dormant state to full awakening.

One of the most beloved and widely worshiped forms of the Goddess is Lakshmi, the consort of Vishnu, who accompanies him in his function of sustaining the universe. She represents all the things we need for a good life: beauty, abundance, good fortune, splendor, generosity, and both material and spiritual wealth. While Mother Kundalini in Her destructive aspect as Kali goes about consuming our dark, poisonous tendencies, She gradually sets our inner being in order. This new sense of interior harmony is a quality of Lakshmi, and it is often reflected outwardly by increased prosperity, abundance, and success in our worldly lives.

Saraswati, the consort of Brahma the Creator, is the goddess of music, knowledge, fluency in speech, and creative inspiration. As we become increasingly purified, clearer and cleaner within, these qualities of Saraswati come to us as Her gifts, culminating in divine wisdom, the knowledge of the Self.

Gurumayi has said:

> We call the Goddess by different names depending on the aspect of Her power we wish to invoke. Shakti is called Saraswati when She gives knowledge and wisdom, when She gives inner experiences of the Truth. She is called Shri Lakshmi when She takes the form of good fortune and abundance. She is called Radha when you experience great devotion, because Radha is the personification of devotion. She is called Durga or Kali when She destroys all that must be destroyed in you, all that is holding you back.[7]

Notes to Chapter 2

1 Swami Muktananda, *Kundalini, The Secret of Life,* 2d edition (New York: SYDA Foundation, 1979), p. 5.

2 A rendering of the *Devī Aparad Kṣamāpana* 3:8.

3 A rendering of *Bhuvaneśvarī* 17, from the *Tantrasāra.*

4 *Śiva Sūtras* 1:13.

5 From an unpublished rendering of *Amritānubhav,* by George Franklin.

6 *Lalitā Sahasranāma* 18, 281.

7 Swami Chidvilasananda, "Creating a Body of Light," *Darshan* magazine 41/42 (1990), p. 163.

Homage to Him who paints the picture of the three worlds, thereby displaying His amazing genius: to Shiva, who is beautiful with the hundreds of appearances laid out by the brush of His own unique, subtle, and pure Shakti.

— Ramakantha, *Spandākārikā Vivritti*

CHAPTER 3

THE DESCENT *of the* SUPREME *into* MATTER

"Shakti, leaping up in delight, lets Herself go forth into manifestation."[1] Shakti creates for the sheer ecstasy of it. As Shakti begins the creative process and streams into manifestation, She assumes progressively denser and grosser forms, in the same way that steam becomes water and solidifies into ice. It is a process of contraction and limitation, known as involution, in which Consciousness becomes involved in nature.

This same process takes place within the human being. Shakti exists in Her limitless, infinite, expansive state in the *sahasrāra*, the highest spiritual center located at the crown of the head. Here Shiva and Shakti are in union. The *sahasrāra* is utterly transcendent, beyond the mind, beyond name and form. When Shakti is in this topmost center, one does not perceive the world; one perceives only all-pervasive light. Yet, even this is merely an attempt to describe the indescribable.

As Shakti begins to descend through the *suṣumnā nāḍī*, the central channel extending from the base of the spine to the crown of the head, She moves into the area of the "Pure Creation" between the *sahasrāra* and the *ājñā* chakra at the space between the eyebrows. As She moves downward through the pure principles of unity-awareness, which are experienced in this region, the world begins to take shape in one's awareness and gradually comes into clearer focus; nevertheless, the subject and object are still perceived as one. The split has not yet occurred.

Right above the *ājñā* chakra, Shakti hits the prism of *māyā* and is refracted through it. Unity-awareness is broken up and dispersed. The subject is severed from the object.

Māyā has been called "the mirror trick that breaks the All into the many." Lord Krishna tells Arjuna: "This divine *māyā* of Mine is difficult to overcome. Those who take refuge in Me alone can overcome it."[2] And Jnaneshwar Maharaj adds that anyone who thinks he can overcome *māyā* by his own efforts is a fool. One can overcome *māyā* by divine grace alone.

Everything is actually one energy; it just appears to be broken up. This is true of the macrocosm (the universe) as well as the microcosm (the human body). Shakti descends into manifestation in progressively denser forms.

As Shakti continues to descend, She reaches the *ājñā chakra*, the center of the four psychic instruments: the mind, the intellect, the ego, and the subconscious mind. Then the gross material elements appear — ether in the *viśuddha chakra* at the throat, air in the *anāhata chakra* at the heart, fire in the *maṇipūra chakra* at the navel, water in the *svādhiṣṭhāna chakra* in the sacral area, and earth in the *mūlādhāra chakra* at the base of the spine.

At this point, a human being is ready for life in the material world, and he is equipped with four different bodies to suit his needs:

(1) The subtlest is the supracausal body or Blue Pearl, a brilliant dot of blue light the size of a lentil seed, in which one experiences the *turīya* or transcendental

state of the Self. Its seat is the *sahasrāra*.

(2) The causal body is represented by a black light the size of a fingertip, in which one experiences the state of deep sleep. Its seat is the heart.

(3) The subtle body may be seen in meditation as a white light the size of a thumb. In this body one experiences the dream state, and its seat is the throat. The subtle body interpenetrates and vitalizes the physical body, and is composed of millions of *nāḍīs*, subtle channels that carry the *prāṇa* throughout the system.

(4) The gross physical body is associated with a red light the same size as the human body, in which one experiences the waking state. Its seat is the eyes. A seeker may see this in meditation as a steady red aura which envelops him inside and outside, and spreads right through him.

Earth, or solid matter, is the last and grossest *tattva*, or principle of creation. The Shakti then stops Her creative activity, and She rests in a coiled form like a serpent. She is now Kundalini Shakti, the Serpent Power, whose dwelling in the human body is in the *mūlādhāra chakra* at the base of the spine. The Sanskrit word *kuṇḍala* means "coiled." Kundalini literally means "that which is coiled." The feminine ending denotes the female aspect of the energy that exists in its coiled, dormant state. Residing in the center of the body, She controls our entire physiological system through the complex network of *nāḍīs*. She is the power behind the mind and the senses and provides the energy for all our activities. The *Ānanda Laharī* says:

> O youthful Spouse of Shiva! You are the mind, ether, air, fire, water, and earth. You have transformed

> Yourself into the universe. Beyond You, there is nothing. In Your play, You manifest Your consciousness and bliss in the form of the universe."[3]

In this outer aspect, Kundalini is always awake; it is Her subtle inner aspect that is dormant and must be awakened.

At this point, at the end of the process of involution, we have completely lost sight of the Self, our divine origin, the pure Consciousness of the *sahasrāra*, and have become engrossed in the outer world of phenomena. We are caught up in the world. We are trapped in the ego, as surely as if we were caught in a web.

The supreme Self is omnipotent, all-powerful. There is nothing it cannot do. The Shaivite scriptures explain that *māyā* throws a series of cloaks over the Self. These cloaks conceal our true identity. They are part of the family of *māyā*, and they limit the powers, or *śaktis*, of Consciousness. These cloaks are called *kañchukas*.

The first *kañchuka* is called *kalā*. This first cloak limits the Supreme's power of omnipotence and shrinks its capacity to act to that of an ordinary human being. In other words, there are some things we can do, and some things we can't do.

The second cloak that *māyā* throws over the Self is called *vidyā*. This limits the Supreme's power of omniscience. This cloak produces limited knowledge in the individual soul. There are some things we know, and there are a lot of things we don't know.

The third cloak is *rāga*. *Rāga* reduces the Supreme's condition of completeness or perfection. We no longer feel whole and entire, sufficient unto ourselves. So this cloak causes desire and love for particular objects. We start looking around for something or someone else who will make us feel complete and whole.

The fourth cloak is *kāla*, which limits the Self's condition of eternal existence. It creates time and the sequential order of things — past, present, and future. This cloak makes us afraid that time is running out. It leads to the fear of aging and of death.

And the fifth and last cloak is *niyati*, which limits the Supreme's all-pervasiveness or omnipresence. We understand that we are here in our own living room; we are not in Bali or Madras.

Is it any wonder that we can't recognize ourselves as the supreme Self? It has shrunk and contracted all its powers, or *śaktis*, and has become a limited individual soul. The scriptures say that in this condition we have *śakti dāridrya*, poverty of Shakti. We wander around in fear and ignorance of who we really are, the Supreme Lord.

This is our plight. Instead of identifying ourselves with our great Self, we identify with our body and our ego. But the scriptures and great beings remind us that if we fully unfold our *śaktis* or powers, we are nothing but supreme Shiva. The human body is actually a storehouse of vast power, and the object of *sādhana* is to raise these various forms of power back to their full expression. We have to retrace our steps and return to our source.

How do we do this? The root of all our latent powers is the Kundalini Shakti. She must be awakened from Her dormant state at the base of the spine and then retrace Her steps, climbing back up through the various principles of creation represented in the *chakras* in the *suṣumnā nāḍī*. This is the process of evolution.

When Kundalini finally becomes established in the *sahasrāra*, the union of Shiva and Shakti takes place. This is *mokṣa*, liberation from the cycle of birth and death, the ultimate goal of human existence. This is why all cultures and spiritual traditions revere and worship Kundalini Shakti; without Her, Shiva cannot be attained. For this reason, the devotee earnestly implores the divine Shakti to set him free from his worldly bonds and afflictions:

O Chandi! Wander in my heart!
Destroy the calamities that besiege me,
Arising from the malice and the fears that pursue me,
So that, free from danger,
And protected by Your lotus feet,
My mind may swim and revel in the ocean of bliss.
O Mother! May showers of holy devotion to You
Always rain upon me,
Struggling and drowning
As I am in the endless ocean of illusion,
Without a taste of the water of
the bliss of the Absolute.[4]

Notes to Chapter 3

1 Kshemaraja, *Śiva Stotrāvalī Ṭīkā*.

2 *Bhagavad Gītā* 7:14.

3 *Ānanda Laharī* 35.

4 A rendering of the *Mahiśarmardinī Stotra* 1 and 7, from the *Tantrasāra*.

That glory is more hidden than the hidden. But when the look of the Guru falls upon one, one is overwhelmed and that glory becomes the most obvious of obvious things.

— Maheshvarananda, *Mahārthamañjarī* 66

CHAPTER 4

THE AWAKENING

The various spiritual traditions employ a wide variety of means to awaken the dormant Kundalini. Some practice severe austerities and fasting, while others recommend concentration techniques involving mantra repetition, chanting, self-inquiry, or solving difficult riddles which short-circuit the mind. Still others make use of complex visualization techniques that involve raising fire up through the *suṣumnā nāḍī*. Also, certain *haṭha yoga āsanas, bandhas,* and types of *prāṇāyāma* force the current of *prāṇa* to enter the *suṣumnā* and awaken Kundalini.

In fact, much of the scriptural literature on Kundalini deals primarily with the problem of waking Her up. People often try to awaken Her through arduous means. A typical example is the following passage from the *Yogakuṇḍalī Upaniṣad:*

> Sitting in the full lotus posture, a wise man should take Kundalini up from Her resting place to the middle of the eyebrows. When the *prāṇa* is passing through the left nostril, he should inhale sixteen digits. Then he should bind the *saraswatī nāḍī* (west of the navel) by means of the lengthened breath, and holding firmly together both his ribs near the navel by means of the thumbs and forefingers of both hands, he should stir up Kundalini with all his

> might from right to left over and over again. He should do this fearlessly for forty-eight minutes.
>
> By this means, Kundalini enters the mouth of the *suṣumnā nāḍī*. Then he should draw himself up a little, compress the neck and expand the navel. Then, by vigorously shaking the *saraswatī nāḍī*, the *prāṇa* goes up through the *suṣumnā* to the chest. By contracting the neck, the *prāṇa* moves upward from the chest.[1]

This is just the beginning. A lengthy section follows, consisting of many different *prāṇāyāma* exercises accompanied by *bandhas*, or locks, to force Kundalini to awaken and rise through the *suṣumnā*. In addition to being difficult and time-consuming, these techniques never carry any guarantee of success and may even be dangerous if performed incorrectly and without expert supervision.

Fortunately, there is an easier way. The scriptures also speak at length of the need for divine grace, which enables a seeker to tread safely this path, which is described as being "as sharp as a razor's edge."

Shaivism speaks explicitly of grace as being one of the five functions performed by supreme Shiva: "I bow to the Divine, who brings about emanation, maintenance, reabsorption, concealment, and who bestows grace, destroying the affliction of those who bow to Him."[2]

Emanation refers to the creation of the universe. Lord Shiva maintains what He has created; then He reabsorbs the creation into Himself. Concealment is the state in which the creation remains within Him in a potential or seed form before being remembered or recreated. Bestowal of grace brings about the complete merging of the creation into the universal consciousness, eradicating all impressions and all opportunities for subsequent remembrance. Grace is the action by which God once again reunites us with Himself.

The Sufis say that the spiritual goal is reached by grace alone and that if you were destined to reach God only after the destruction of your faults and the abandonment of all your claims, you would never reach Him.

Becoming more explicit, the *Śiva Sūtra Vimarśinī* states that the Guru is the grace-bestowing power of God. It is the Guru who functions as the instrument through which the Divine bestows grace, which occurs by means of a process known as *dīkṣā*, or initiation.

Another Shaivite scripture explains: "*Dīkṣā* grants realization and destroys all impurities. It is called *dīkṣā* because it imparts that realization that awakens one from the sleep of ignorance. It has the characteristics of both giving *(dī)* and destroying *(kṣa)*."[3]

The *yoga sūtras* on *śaktipāt* (literally, "the descent of Shakti") go on to say that *śaktipāt* alone is initiation, that *śaktipāt* happens only through the grace of the Guru, and that during *śaktipāt* the Guru transmits the Shakti into the seeker.[4] The Guru throws sparks of divine fire into the disciple, and they in turn ignite the seeker's own dormant Kundalini Shakti.

Baba Muktananda said:

> Many lesser teachers can effect a partial awakening, but Kundalini soon becomes dormant again, leaving the seeker in an anxious state. A lot of people who met me during my world tours said, "My Kundalini was awakened three years ago, but now it is asleep again." This is what happens when one does not have the grace of a perfected Master, and such an awakening does not serve much purpose. Only a Guru who has received the blessing of the Supreme Goddess and his own Guru and who has received the command to perform *śaktipāt*, can bring about a

> permanent awakening that can take the seeker to the final goal.[5]

A noted Indian scholar, M. P. Pandit, says:

> Whatever the path chosen and discipline selected for the seeker, no real *sādhana* begins till a relation is established between him and the Guru. And this relation starts from the moment an inner connection is made between the two as a result of something from the consciousness of the Guru entering into the being of the disciple. This entry of the Guru into the disciple is aptly described as the impact or descent of the higher Power, the conscious Power of the Guru, or of the very Divine through him: *śaktipāt*. Where this *śaktipāt* is not, say the scriptures, there is no fulfillment.[6]

The four ways in which the Guru classically gives *śaktipāt* are through a physical touch (*sparśa dīkṣā*), word (*mantra dīkṣā*), thought or will (*saṅkalpa* or *mānasa dīkṣā*), and look (*drik dīkṣā*).

Sparśa Dīkṣā: Initiation by Touch

The Guru can give *śaktipāt* by touch in a variety of ways: perhaps through a brush of a wand of peacock feathers, or the Guru may lay his or her hand on a seeker's head, press the point between his eyebrows, or touch him on the back. Even a casual touch from the Guru can awaken the inner Shakti.

One woman said that after Gurumayi touched her head during an Intensive she had a vision in meditation that her whole head had opened up. The top of her head "exploded," and all around her there was a gorgeous blue-black sky studded with stars. She felt an indescribable peace. A gentle, serpentine energy was moving very slowly at the base of her neck, creating waves of ecstasy throughout her whole body. She lost all sense of time. The following day, during meditation, a bolt of energy soared up through her. She felt her heart burst open and she began to sob and laugh at the same time. Then the serpentine energy turned into a shaft of pure white light and shot up through the top of her head. Suddenly, she found herself at the center of the universe. All things were her and she was all things. And all of time, from the beginning to the end, was apparent to her, was in her, and of her. She began to cry with joy, understanding that all her years of study, of searching, and of longing, had been for this.

Sometimes the Shakti is transmitted through an object that the Guru has touched; the Shakti is contagious. Baba used to have a beautiful, sleek Rottweiler named Madhu, who lived in Baba's house. He was enormously fond of Madhu and would often pet him and stroke him with great affection. It's not surprising that Madhu was permeated with Shakti. At one point, when Madhu was under the weather, a veterinarian was called in. As he began to examine Madhu, he felt a bolt of energy pass into him and he began to experience tremors. Mystified, the vet wanted to know what was going on. So Baba's attendant had to explain to him about Kundalini, *śaktipāt*, and the Guru, right there on the spot.

Baba loved this story and often chuckled about it. One day he called me and told me to put it in my next Kundalini talk. "But," Baba added, "be sure you tell people that this doesn't mean that Madhu was the veterinarian's Guru!"

Mantra Dīkṣā: Initiation by Word

Śaktipāt can also be given through the Guru's mantra. The mantra given by a Siddha Guru is a *chaitanya* mantra, one that is alive with conscious force, as opposed to a *jaḍa*, an inert, mantra that one might select from a book or hear from a friend. The Guru received the mantra from his or her own Guru and has attained realization through fully unfolding its power. Behind it is the Shakti of the entire lineage of Siddhas, and that Shakti is passed on to the disciple through the syllables of the mantra.

One man received a mantra card in response to a letter he had written Baba. He sat for meditation and started repeating *Oṁ Namaḥ Śivāya.* He became very relaxed and found the mantra drawing his awareness into some deep, empty space inside himself. At one point he stopped repeating the mantra, but it immediately began repeating itself within him. The reverberation of *Oṁ Namaḥ Śivāya* got stronger and stronger until he was engulfed in the ocean of the mantra's vibration. Then, an explosion took place. His awareness, his sense of who and what he was, began expanding infinitely in every direction until there was nothing in the universe that he was not. There was an inconceivable ecstasy. Then, he became aware of a screen on which hundreds of images were passing by in rapid-fire fashion. He realized that what he was seeing was the screen of his own mind. The images were of everything stored away in his mind, from this lifetime and many other lifetimes in the past. Yet, in his blissful state of infinite Consciousness, he knew that his existence was totally separate from that of the mind he was witnessing.

My own experience of *śaktipāt* happened through the mantra. I began to visit one of Baba's meditation centers in California in 1972. Within a week after I started using Baba's mantra, I had a very powerful experience. In meditation, I saw a rectangle of brilliant white light approaching me. When it reached the space between my eyebrows, I felt a tremendous pressure and suddenly everything burst into white light. There was no more "me," as I had always thought of myself — there was only light, which felt like the essence of everything. After a short time, the light condensed back into a rectangle, which moved away and vanished. Then Baba appeared and explained that this had been my "*dīkṣā*," a word I had never heard before. He showed me the image of a tubular fireman's chute. I saw that I had just been put into the top of the chute and that from then on, no matter what I did, I would very naturally reach the bottom and exit into safety and freedom. I came out of this experience with a tremendous pressure at the *ājñā chakra*, which continued unabated for two weeks. This was the beginning of a fascinating process.

Saṅkalpa or Mānasa Dīkṣā: Initiation by Will or Thought

Sometimes the Guru gives *śaktipāt* through will, thought, or intention. Because the Guru principle is all-pervasive, the Guru does not have to be physically present in order to do this. Years ago in Gurudev Siddha Peeth, a man went up to Baba and showed him a photograph of a group of people. He pointed to a particular woman in the photo and said, "Baba, this is my wife. Could you please give her *śaktipāt*?" Baba studied the photograph for a few moments and then said, "Yes, she will get it in three days." Several weeks later the man received a letter from his wife, who was at their home in California. A curious thing had happened to her, she said. She had been washing dishes at her kitchen sink one day when she was suddenly gripped by a powerful force and her body began to perform spontaneous *haṭha yoga* postures. She asked her husband to tell Baba about it and ask for his advice and blessings. The husband realized from her description that they were physical *kriyās*, movements of the body impelled by the awakened energy. And this had occurred three days after he had shown Baba her photograph.

Mānasa dīkṣā is probably the most frequent way *śaktipāt* is given in the Siddha Yoga Meditation Intensives. Even when Gurumayi is not physically present, she can awaken the Shakti in this way.

Drik Dīkṣā: Initiation by Look

The Guru may transmit the Shakti to the seeker through a look or glance. Or the seeker may receive *śaktipāt* by looking at the Guru, either directly or at a photograph or other image.

An English couple had a housekeeper who never met Gurumayi. In fact, although she regularly cleaned their meditation room and saw the many pictures of Gurumayi, Baba, and Bade Baba in their house, she never referred to them and never asked about them. They in turn did not discuss meditation with her, as they did not know what her beliefs were. Several years ago they went to South Fallsburg to spend time with Gurumayi. On their return, their housekeeper told them that while they were away, she was cleaning their bedroom. She was dusting a cupboard that contained some videos of talks by Gurumayi. One of the videos was entitled "The Self Reveals Itself," and it seemed to jump out at her. She thought that she would take a look at it, and she watched the talk. At the end of the video Gurumayi gives some meditation instructions, and the housekeeper thought that she would try to see if she could meditate for just a up, overcome by a sense of the divine and filled with awe. And I resolved never again to underestimate *śaktip*… It is the most significant moment of a person's life.

Gurumayi speaks of *śaktipāt*: "When the ascent c… disciple's love meets the descent of the Guru's lo… eternal bond is formed in the heart. Without th… there is no true relationship with the inner Sel… of us who have received this great and divir… ize that we were never truly alive before.

The scriptures caution that it is the G… not just to awaken the Shakti; he or she … trol its functioning thereafter. This is o… est mysteries of the Guru and of the … under the guidance of such a bein… asked Baba how this was possibl… case of his many thousands of d… able to spend much time arou… Baba replied:

> The Shakti pervades the … to west, from north to south, a… hasn't spared anyone. Although a disc… far away from me, the Shakti is the same th… well as here. I have to lose myself in the Shakti; only then does the Shakti work everywhere for everyone. It is all-pervasive, but I have the switch to turn it on....
>
> When a being loses himself in the light, he becomes a perfect Guru. God is of the form of divine light. If I lose myself in that light, then I have perfection and complete Guruhood. When we worship a Guru, we don't worship his physical body. We worship him with the awareness that he is the supreme and all-pervasive light.[11]

minute or two, as she had never done it before. She closed her eyes and almost immediately felt a powerful surge of energy running through her body. It seemed to start at the base of her spine and when it rose up to her head, she began to see hundreds of brilliant lights. Her breathing became very shallow and fast, and she kept seeing the brilliant lights and feeling the energy in her body.

Eventually, after how long she didn't know, she opened her eyes and her gaze locked on to a photograph of Gurumayi on the dresser to her left.

She decided to go out for some air, and she went downstairs and opened the door. Everything outside seemed to be sparkling. All the trees and leaves and grass were so beautiful, and she felt such a feeling of love and happiness — she had never experienced anything like it before. She wished that everyone in the world could experience what she was feeling. It was so incredible.

Baba Muktananda tells us in his autobiography, *Play of Consciousness*, that he received *śaktipāt* through *drik dīkṣā* from his Guru, Bhagawan Nityananda. Baba says:

> He looked into my eyes once more. I watched him very attentively. A ray of light was coming from his pupils, and going right inside me. Its touch was searing, red-hot, and its brilliance dazzled my eyes like a high-powered bulb. As this ray flowed from Bhagawan Nityananda's eyes into my own, the very hair on my body rose in wonder, awe, ecstasy, and fear. I went on...watching the colors of this ray. It was an unbroken stream of divine radiance. Sometimes it was the color of molten gold, sometimes saffron, sometimes a deep blue, more lustrous than a shining star. I stood there, stunned, watching the brilliant rays passing into me....[7]

Afterward, as Baba was walking home, he exper…

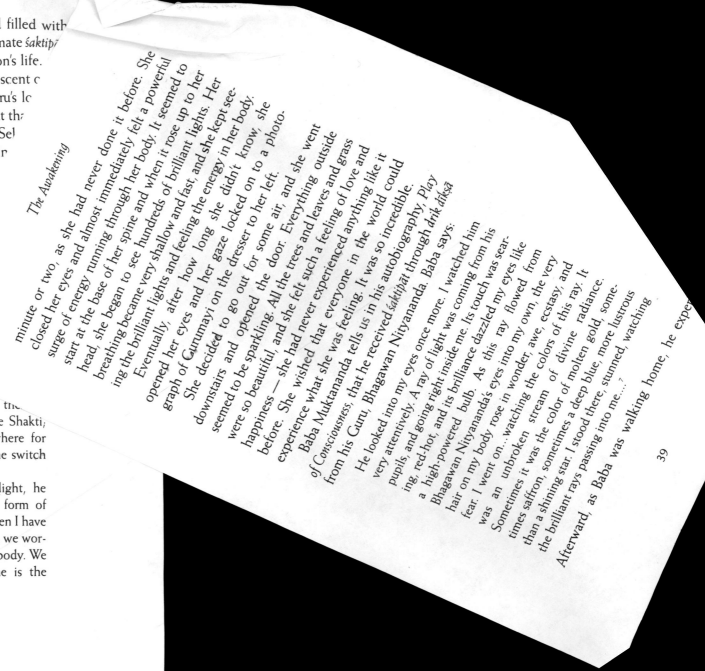

Notes to Chapter 4

1 *Yogakuṇḍalī Upaniṣad*, Chapter 1.

2 *Svacchanda Tantra* 1:3.

3 Utpalabhatta, *Spanda Pradīpikā* 3:7.

4 Swami Vishnu Tīrtha Maharaj, *Śaktipāt — Kundalini Mahayoga* (Sanskrit/Hindi edition; Devas, Madhya Pradesh: Sri Sadhan Granthamala Prakashan Samiti, Narayana Kuti, Sannyas Ashram), 2:5, 4:8, and 1:7.

5 Swami Muktananda, *Kundalini, The Secret of Life*, 2d edition (New York: SYDA Foundation, 1979), p. 26.

6 M. P. Pandit, *Studies in the Tantras and the Veda* (India: Sterling Publishers, 1988).

7 Swami Muktananda, *Play of Consciousness*, translated by Swami Chidvilasananda, 3d printing, 1987 (New York: SYDA Foundation, 1974), p. 65.

8 Ibid., pp. 69-70.

9 Swami Muktananda, *In the Company of a Siddha*, revised edition (New York: SYDA Foundation, 1985), p. 127.

10 Swami Chidvilasananda, unpublished talk, August 14, 1985.

11 *In the Company of a Siddha*, p. 132.

---

the outer world...

He says:

I repeatedly opened and
shut them I saw innumerable club
rays and millions of tiny twinkling spark
within me. I kept watching them. What a beau-
sight! Those infinitely small sparks were shimmering and coursing through my whole body at an
incredible speed. I looked with wonder and awe at
their speed and their number. Then I opened my
eyes again. Again there were masses of the same
tiny, scintillating, blue sparks coruscating around
me. I was overcome with awe and ecstasy.... Even
today I can remember that experience of oneness. I
still see those tiny blue dots.[8]

Once someone asked Baba if Kundalini could be
awakened accidentally. "Yes," he replied laughing, "but
only if an 'accident' takes place between a Guru and a
disciple... When a disciple who is full of devotion
meets a Guru who is saturated with Shakti, Kundalini is
awakened immediately."[9]

Because those who live in the Ashram see so many
people receiving *śaktipāt*, sometimes we begin to take
this great gift for granted. This happened to me a few
years ago. During this time I had a dream in which
Baba and Gurumayi appeared to me and said, "You must
understand the greatness of *śaktipāt*." Then they showed
me what happens at the moment the Guru transmits
the Shakti into a seeker. I saw that it was God's energy
entering the person and filling him with light. I woke

It is difficult to describe in words the experience I had when His grace flowed into my heart, into my mind, and into my eyes. My frame swelled to immense proportions. He broke the cage that had imprisoned my soul and released me from the numerous principles of creation. My eyes drank His light in full and I lived in His grace.

—Tirumular

CHAPTER 5

THE IMPACT *of* THE DIVINE POWER

Why do people react differently to *śaktipāt*? It is a question of our *saṃskāras*, or past impressions. The *yoga sūtras* on *śaktipāt* say, "*Kriyās* occur, not because of the will, but because of the *saṃskāras*."[1]

We retain all the subtle impressions of our past experiences throughout countless lifetimes, and these experiences of course differ from one person to another. These impressions, or *saṃskāras*, are both positive and negative and are what compel us to act and react in certain set patterns of behavior. They are the cause of our mental and emotional conditioning. Our *saṃskāras* determine how we react to *śaktipāt* — the intensity with which we receive it and the types of *kriyās* that it produces.

For this reason, even though the Guru bestows grace equally on all his or her disciples, the result is never exactly the same. If the Guru's Shakti enters a seeker who is pure and whose *saṃskāras* have been weakened through previous *sādhana*, it will work in him very quickly. If all his *nāḍīs* (subtle channels through which the *prāṇa* or life-force flows) are pure and clear, he will receive Shakti with the greatest force. Conversely, if a seeker has done very little *sādhana* or none at all, if his *saṃskāras* are strong and unyielding, and if his system is full of impurities, it will take the Shakti a long time to do its job. This is why people react very differently to *śaktipāt*.

One day a seeker asked Baba, "When you give *śaktipāt* to us at an Intensive, do you give it to us in the same way and with the same strength that your Guru, Bhagawan Nityananda, gave it to you?" Baba replied, "The question is, do you receive it the way I received it?"

A person receives as much as he can hold. The great saint Ramana Maharshi once said that the grace of the Guru is like the ocean. If a seeker comes with a cup, he or she will receive only a cupful. There is no use complaining that the ocean is miserly. The bigger the vessel a seeker brings, the more he will be able to take away. It is entirely up to him.

During an evening program some years ago, a woman prayed intensely to Baba for a higher state of consciousness. As she was riding home after the program, she began to experience dizziness. She opened the car window to get some fresh air. Suddenly, she said, she was catapulted into an exalted state. But she realized it was like throwing a supercharge of electricity into a little twenty-five-watt bulb: she was not yet equipped to handle it.

The power of the Shakti is like fire. One has to be able to withstand it. The higher states of consciousness will come at the right time — when one's body has become strong and pure enough to hold the tremendous force of the Shakti.

As Dante wrote, "Throughout all the universe God's ray enters all things according to their merit, and nothing has the power to block its way."[2]

Abhinavagupta, the great tenth-century Siddha and master of tantra, yoga, philosophy, and the arts of poetry and drama, wrote numerous works on the philosophy of Kashmir Shaivism, among which are his *Tantrāloka* and *Tantrasāra*. In these works he discusses the varying intensity and types of *śaktipāt*. He has broadly analyzed the nature of *śaktipāt* according to three types: (1) *tīvra*, very intense; (2) *madhya*, of moderate intensity; and (3) *manda*, of low intensity. He has further broken down each of these categories into three subgroups, which he discusses one by one. He adds at the end that each of these nine types of *śaktipāt* can in turn be broken down into three additional subgroups, bringing the number to twenty-seven, and then each of these can also be further categorized into many subsidiary types.[3]

(1) A person who receives *tīvra-tīvra* (the most intense variety of intense *śaktipāt*) attains spontaneous knowledge of the Self and instantaneous liberation. He immediately understands that the pure, limitless, and blissful Consciousness is his own Self, and he sees everything as a reflection appearing in that Consciousness. However, the force of the Shakti is so intense in this form of initiation that his system cannot withstand it, and he soon leaves his body. He becomes a Master in the subtle realms.

(2) A person who receives *tīvra-madhya śaktipāt* (still intense but less so) also experiences a spontaneous realization of the Self, but he does not leave his body. He remains in this world as a Master for the upliftment of mankind.

(3) A person who receives *tīvra-manda śaktipāt* (the slowest variety within the intense category) does not experience spontaneous realization, so he must find a Guru. He attains the highest state through the Guru's look, word, thought, or touch. Through

these first three degrees of intense *śaktipāt*, Lord Shiva creates Masters. With the less intense varieties of *śaktipāt*, He creates disciples.

(4) A person who receives *madhya-tīvra* (the strongest of the moderate degrees of *śaktipāt*) goes to a Master, but a touch or a glance of the Master will not enlighten him. The Guru initiates him into a mantra and teaches him how to follow the spiritual path. He fully attains his divine nature only when he leaves his physical body.

(5) In the *madhya-madhya* degree of *śaktipāt*, a person has an intense desire for Self-realization; however, he also retains some desire for worldly pleasures. When he leaves his body, he goes to a celestial realm to experience the pleasures there until he is fully satisfied. He receives initiation once again in that realm, and there he merges into Shiva.

(6) A person who receives the *madhya-manda* degree of *śaktipāt* has a greater desire for worldly pleasures than he does for Self-realization. When he leaves his physical body, he goes to a celestial realm to satisfy his longing for enjoyment. Then he must take birth again on earth as a *yoga brasṭha,* one who has practiced yoga but was unable to complete his *sādhana* in his previous lifetime. He continues his spiritual practice and attains perfection in this birth.

(7-9) A person who receives the *manda,* or least intense, variety of *śaktipāt* has a strong attachment to worldly life. He yearns to attain Self-realization only when things go badly for him. At that time he may decide to renounce everything and dedicate himself exclusively to spiritual practice, but he is unable to sustain it. He attains liberation in stages by taking birth in some higher world and then returns to this physical world to live out all his karmas and desires. This occurs over and over again until he eventually attains the highest state.

Abhinavagupta says:

> When one follows the path of the transcendental Reality by adhering to the teachings of the Guru, one suddenly becomes Shiva Himself as a result of extremely intense *śaktipāt*. Another person climbs the ladder of the *tattvas* step by step, reaches the ultimate Principle, and finally identifies himself as Shiva. But a person who stops midway in his meditation and does not reach the supreme Reality is called a *yoga braṣṭha* by the scriptures. When he dies he becomes a lord in the worlds of pleasure, and due to the effect of the stage of meditation he attained, he will reach Shiva in a later birth.[4]

Sometimes when people hear about the varying degrees of *śaktipāt*, their immediate reaction is to become discouraged over how impure they are and how slow their progress is. Fortunately, however, the Shakti meets us wherever we happen to be along the spiritual path and then moves us along from there. It is the task of the Shakti to purify us, so no matter how impure and blocked we may think we are, the Shakti will gradually remove those impurities and uplift us. We can cooperate with Her by doing the practices — meditation, chanting, repetition of the mantra, selfless service — and by living a life of discipline and moderation. In this way, our vessel is purified and strengthened so it can hold the tremendous power of the Shakti.

Abhinavagupta says, "Just as a face clearly appears in a spotless mirror, in the same way, the Self shines in all its splendor in the mind purified by Shiva's *śaktipāt*."[5]

Baba once said, "I give you a divine spark; now it is your job to convert that spark into a forest fire." Our spiritual practices fan the flames of Kundalini so that She blazes with great brilliance.

A woman I have known for many years received *śaktipāt* from Baba and immediately began to have dramatic experiences of inner music, visions of light, and powerful currents of energy streaming through her body. Her husband was intrigued and signed up for an Intensive. Apparently nothing happened to him — at least not the standard signs he was looking for. But he was regular in his practices; every evening he and his wife would sit together for meditation in a beautiful room they had set aside for spiritual practice. It was always the same — his wife would meditate and have wonderful experiences, while he would sit and listen to his mind chatter away. After a while, when he couldn't stand it any longer, he would get up and busy himself with household chores, repairing the kitchen sink or resurfacing the floor.

A few months later he decided to take a second Intensive, and then a third — but things stayed more or less the same. No noticeable experiences, no deep meditation. Yet he still kept sitting every evening without fail. Then one night his body suddenly moved into physical *kriyās*, with powerful *bandhas* and *prāṇāyāmas*. At last, a concrete sign that Kundalini was awake in him!

What had happened? Baba used to say that some people are like wet logs. When fire is set to a piece of wood that is green or damp, it must first dry out the wood before it can blaze. In the same way, in many people the Shakti functions very subtly for some time, doing Her initial work of preparing the system for the more intense forms of manifestation later on.

Each seeker must begin his spiritual journey from where he stopped in his previous life. Baba once used the analogy of eating lunch and then taking a nap: when we wake up our lunch is still in our stomach. In the same way, if we do *sādhana* but die before reaching the final goal, we will begin our next life with whatever level of attainment we achieved in our former lifetime.

A few years ago, a nine-year-old boy came to the South Fallsburg Ashram with his parents. He immediately began having visions of various kinds even with his eyes open, traveled to different galaxies, and saw scenes from previous lifetimes. Another little boy, age eight, came to Gurudev Siddha Peeth from his home in Bombay, and his mother took him to the meditation hall in Turiya Mandir. When he sat to meditate, he said, a powerful force began to rise from the base of his spine with a serpentine motion through a number of different centers. When it reached his throat there was an explosion of light, and then a small snake continued to rise on up to the crown of his head. Afterward, he made a watercolor painting of his vision, showing the *chakras* with the *suṣumnā*, the central channel, and the *īḍā* and *piṅgalā nāḍīs* on either side of it.

These experiences were not accidental; they were the result of yogic practice in a previous birth. These two young boys were undoubtedly *yoga braṣṭhas*, and their accumulated merit and *sādhana* were now bearing fruit in this lifetime. As soon as they entered the Ashram, the Shakti caught them with great force.

Some people complain that God or the Guru is partial and gives more grace to some than to others. But the Shaivite philosophers point out that, in the first place, the whole question of bondage versus liberation exists only as a concept in the mind. Since there is nothing in the universe that is not Shiva, how could God be partial or impartial to Himself? The appearance of bondage and liberation is merely His play on the stage of His own being.

Although we can make certain generalizations about grace, its functioning remains a divine mystery. Usually it depends on a person's receptivity. The Guru is like the sun, which sheds its light equally on all; but if we go inside a building or stand under a tree, the sun's rays will not touch us. Nevertheless, there are some people who have to seek grace for a long time before it is granted to them. The poet-saint Kabir had to go to great lengths in order to receive Ramananda's grace. He concealed himself in Ramananda's path so the Guru would step on him and call out the mantra in surprise. On the other hand, there are many cases where grace descends on a person who apparently is not the slightest bit interested and who is not consciously seeking it.

Again, the Shaivite philosophers remind us that there is no scope for any kind of "why" in a state of absolute independence. If God were stripped of His independence, He would cease to be God. He is simply manifesting this play of bondage and liberation in accordance with His unlimited will.

Notes to Chapter 5

1 Swami Vishnu Tirtha Maharaj, *Śaktipāt — Kundalini Mahayoga* (Sanskrit/Hindi edition; Devas, Madhya Pradesh: Shri Sadhan Granthamala Prakashan Samiti Narayana Kuti, Sannyas Ashram) 4:12.

2 Dante, *Paradiso*, Canto 31.

3 See Swami Lakshman Jee, *Kashmir Śaivism, The Secret Supreme* (New York: The Universal Shaiva Trust, 1988), pp. 66-70.

4 *Paramārthasāra* 96-99.

5 Ibid., 9.

When the Kundalini Shakti is awakened, those devotees should not be considered ordinary. They comprehend unseen things, their bodies throb and tremble, their voices choke with tears of love, and they are filled with bliss. When fire enters iron, it does not remain just iron. Similarly, when Kundalini Shakti awakens in human beings, they do not remain mere human beings. They become filled with divine love, divine powers, and divine virtues.

— *Vāyavīya Saṁhitā* 2:11, 35-39

CHAPTER 6

THE UNFOLDING

Once Kundalini is awakened, She begins the enormous task that awaits Her — removing all the obstacles and impurities that lie in Her path, cleaning our inner house from top to bottom. In fact, soon after I received *śaktipāt*, this was a vision that would recur now and then in my meditations:

I had been given a small house to live in, which was charming but quite dirty. I set to work doing what I could with a dust cloth and vacuum cleaner. Then an army of serpents — very friendly ones — would arrive to help me with the deep work that lay beyond my reach. One of them would slither into the bathtub, another into the toilet, a third into the lavatory, and a fourth into the kitchen sink. They would turn into serpentine "Roto-Rooters," scouring out the deep subconscious *saṃskāras* lurking under the surface of my awareness. All of this kicked up a tremendous amount of dust and grime, and for a while it made an awful mess. But eventually the chaos subsided, and I was left with a glistening little house, freshly scrubbed and much more pleasant to live in.

The yogic scriptures explain that the *saṃskāras* are stored inside the *suṣumnā nāḍī*, and when Kundalini awakes and enters the *suṣumnā*, She begins to dislodge and expel them.

A man described an experience he had in meditation of this process of purification. He was in a beautiful walled garden on a huge estate. He was the owner of that place, and he was weeding the garden, parts of which were tremendously overgrown. He began to clear away a beautiful path that led to a high stone wall covered with weeds. This took a while. Everything had to be cleared, up to and including the wall. When he started pulling down the vines and ivies, he saw, much to his surprise, that underneath them was a huge, beautiful, double wooden door that had been completely concealed. After struggling for a while, he was finally able to open it. When the doors swung open, he stood there in astonishment. Outside the wall, in exact alignment with the path he had just cleared, was a road that went all the way out to infinity, and into an incredible panorama of blue light. It was a living blue light. A humming sound, an angelic *Oṁ*, emanated from it and filled him with awe.

Baba Muktananda said:

> Whatever thoughts one has come from the central *nāḍī*, and all one's karmas and impressions from many lives are lodged here. All the different states we experience — desire or greed, inspiration or dullness — arise from the *suṣumnā*. In the upper region of the *suṣumnā* are such qualities as contentment, peace, and knowledge, while in the lower regions lie the passions of lust, greed, anger, and all the feelings of insecurity and inadequacy. When your Shakti is awakened, all the past impressions and karmas come out. That is why when you first receive *śaktipāt*, you sometimes feel very negative or very angry. You shouldn't be afraid when you get into such a state; it happens because the Shakti is expelling all the karmas of countless lives.[1]

While the *saṃskāras* are being removed, they rise into our awareness and we experience them, sometimes with great intensity. If our mind has a tendency to become agitated, for example, our agitation may seem to get worse for a while. If we have a problem with fear, our fearfulness may increase temporarily. We must understand that this process is beneficial, however, and that the Shakti is cutting away at the very roots of our tendencies. At these times the best thing to do is witness the process, with gratitude that these things are being eliminated from our system. Indulging the *saṃskāras*, acting them out, judging them, or repressing them — these approaches are not helpful. Kundalini will expel the tendencies from our system in due course. Meanwhile, we can cooperate with the process by simply witnessing it.

There is no way to predict what will happen next, or when. The awakened Kundalini Shakti usually does not purify all the *chakras* in a linear sequence. Most often She skips around, working in one area for a while, then in another. You never know when the most sublime experience awaits you.

Early one morning I was sitting for meditation in my room, when my alarm rang to announce that it was time to go downstairs for *chai*, spiced tea, before the recitation of the *Guru Gītā*. I was halfway to my feet when, suddenly, I had a vision in which the crown of my head opened to reveal a dazzling white lotus of a thousand petals — the *sahasrāra*! It was exquisite. The petals were alive and pulsing with energy; they resembled whirring wings. I gazed at it in amazement and promptly sat down again. I decided not to be in such a hurry!

The awakened Kundalini Shakti unites with the *prāṇa*, the vital force, and streams through the entire subtle and physical system. The subtle body is a body of energy or light interpenetrating the physical body. It is the seat of the mind and the emotions, and is the body in which we experience our dream state. It is composed of millions of *nāḍīs*, subtle conduits that carry the *prāṇa*. The Shakti purifies all the *nāḍīs* and strengthens the body. The blockages and impurities in the *nāḍīs* are what produce the imbalances in our system and are responsible for our physical and mental disorders. Once Kundalini gets rid of these blocks, our mind is purified and our negative tendencies and patterns leave us permanently. The *yoga sūtras* on *śaktipāt* describe the effects of this process: "One becomes intoxicated with divine feelings and becomes free from anger and other negativities."[2]

As the *saṃskāras* are eliminated, we notice a corresponding transformation of our inner state, which in turn is reflected in our outer lives. Old bad habits and addictions fall away. Our creative abilities are unleashed, and we receive guidance and insight from within. One woman said that at the end of the first year after her *śaktipāt* experience, she was a different person. She completed her doctoral thesis and several other books, and she had stopped smoking. She said there was order in her house and order within herself. She got along much better with other people. And, above all, she never again felt the anguish and loneliness that had characterized her inner state for so many years.

We find that our anger diminishes, and we stay centered in times of stress. One man said that before he met Baba he had been a professional hockey player. He had played hockey from the age of three. He described it as a tough, violent game and said that in order to play you need some aggressiveness, some anger, and a bit of violence. When he went to Miami to spend the winter with Baba, his seva was in the kitchen, chopping vegetables. While he was chopping, something strange happened — he could feel waves of anger. They would rush through his body, and sometimes they were so strong that he would actually see red in front of his eyes. He remembered Baba saying that when an emotion like anger comes up, don't act on it, just witness it. So that's what he did. He just watched it. During the four months he spent with Baba, a great deal of the anger that he had accumulated in his life playing hockey was expelled by the Shakti.

As a result of experiencing the Self, our perception of ourselves and of others changes. We identify less with our ego and more with our higher Self. A woman who lived in Gurudev Siddha Peeth for some time said that it became her habit to go up on the Ashram roof after the morning *Guru Gītā* chant to watch the sun come up and experience a few moments of solitude. One morning she was surveying the landscape, when she fell into a meditative state. She suddenly became aware that a presence — other than what she usually thought of as herself — was looking through her eyes. This presence was an infinite, dispassionate awareness that was simply seeing without judging or analyzing what it saw. It was so compelling that her attention was forcibly drawn to it. She became aware that it was also hearing through her ears; in fact, it was functioning through all her senses. Her entire body was pervaded with that Consciousness; it was the very essence of her life. She lost herself in this experience. She understood that this Consciousness was absolutely changeless, eternal, and infinite. The state accompanying this experience was entirely free from anxiety, need, and expectation.

Gradually, she began to regain awareness of the world around her. She was looking out at a small hill in the distance, and she could see that on the hill there were trees and small bushes. She suddenly realized that if no one had ever told her that the tree was different from the hill, and that the bush was different from both of them, it never would have occurred to her to separate them. She would have considered them all to be parts of the same thing, a unified whole. She realized that by giving names to certain forms, we ourselves create the many out of the One. She perceived that this dispassionate, eternal Consciousness was functioning through the bodies of every living creature. In fact, the entire world was its body. It was seeing itself through every eye, and hearing its sounds through every ear. She understood that all perception of difference is the mind's creation.

After some time the experience subsided, and she came down from the roof. In the days that followed, she realized that her entire outlook had undergone a radical transformation. Before, she had been a very judgmental person. She thought some people were high and others low, some great and others small. But now, everywhere she looked she saw only equality. Each person was an embodiment of that one immutable Consciousness.

After *śaktipāt* we may find a growing capacity to love unconditionally, and our depression may gradually disappear. A Shaivite scripture says, "The ignorant man does not observe the most precious wealth lying in his body, and feels overwhelming depression in his heart. If the Supreme Goddess, who delights in bringing into being the entire universe, enters his heart, then She reduces to ashes the depression that had been plaguing him."[3] A woman came to Gurumayi, saying that her life was falling apart. Her marriage of fifteen years was on the rocks, and her dream home was about to be snatched away from her. After the woman took an Intensive and received *śaktipāt*, she said that a shift took place. For the first time in her life, she had a sense of something deep inside her that did not need any outer support. She knew that as long as she remained anchored in that center, she could meet any calamity that life might bring her with courage and detachment.

As the awakened energy moves us through personal limitations, we gradually become fearless. When we come to understand and trust the Shakti, we gain the ability to let go and allow things to flow naturally. We become free from our anxieties and our tendency to worry all the time.

After her Kundalini was awakened, one woman said, she was able to talk to her mother for the first time in twenty years. And a painter managed to produce enough paintings in the first six weeks following *śaktipāt* for an entire show because the blocks had been removed from his creative expression.

As Baba has said:

> For this awakening, you do not have to abandon your normal pursuits. Do not think that daily life goes against the pursuit of God. If this beautiful, vast world were against God-realization, God would not have created it. God created this variegated cosmos for His own delight, to honor Himself, to create a place where He could revel in His glory. So you can visit that divine place inside while living your normal life; you can visit it again and again, any number of times.[4]

When the divine Shakti awakens within us, She increases our spiritual capacities. She gives us a new interest in spiritual life and the ability to meditate. Our cravings diminish and a previously unknown detachment is born in us. We become deeply content and serene.

For this reason, the ancient sages worshiped the Shakti and prayed for Her help and Her constant presence in their lives. There is a beautiful prayer in the *Rig Veda* that says, "O Almighty Lord, may we, armed with Your powerful divine Shakti, completely annihilate our inner vices in the struggles of life and be victorious."[5]

Because the *saṃskāras* embedded in the *suṣumnā* differ from one individual to another, people's reactions to *śaktipāt* vary greatly in intensity, as we have already seen. They also vary in terms of the specific form they take. The *yoga sūtras* on *śaktipāt* list four broad classifications of *śaktipāt* according to the ways in which it manifests. They are *kriyāvati*, *kalāvati*, *varṇamayī*, and *vedhamayī*.[6]

Kriyāvati

Kriyāvati manifests as *kriyās*, movements of the physical body caused by the awakened energy, and it is associated with *haṭha yoga*. A person may spontaneously perform *āsanas* or postures, *bandhas* or locks, *mudrās* or hand gestures, and *prāṇāyāma* or breathing processes. He does not do these things intentionally; they happen through the force of the awakened Kundalini. In fact, the whole science of *haṭha yoga* was developed by the sages' observations of those who were experiencing a *kriyāvati* type of awakening. They discovered that a careful and systematic duplication of those postures could help to awaken Kundalini in others.

In order to avoid complications, however, a person should attempt these practices only under the guidance of a Master. When these postures and locks occur automatically as the result of receiving *śaktipāt* from a Siddha Guru, they are completely safe. Their occurrence shows that they are necessary for the purification of the system.

A young man who was a professional dancer contracted rheumatoid arthritis at the age of nineteen. By twenty-two he was unable to continue his career, and when he was twenty-four he walked with a cane and was stooped over. He had been to many hospitals and had taken many drugs to get rid of his pain and suffering, but to no avail.

At this point he received *śaktipāt* and felt a bolt of energy enter him right between his eyebrows. As it began to circulate throughout his whole body, powerful physical *kriyās* took place. His legs locked into the lotus posture, he started bouncing up and down like a frog, and every joint in his body began to crack. His back lurched backward and his head bent back all the way to the floor.

After about four months, he could straighten up his body. After six months, he put his cane away. His horrible ordeal was over, and he was completely healthy again.

The *bandhas,* or locks, stabilize the *prāṇa*, cleanse the *nāḍīs*, and still the mind for meditation. The three locks are *mūla bandha,* where the heel locks itself against the anus, forcing it to contract; *uḍḍiyāna bandha,* in which the breath is expelled and the stomach is drawn in; and the *jālandhara bandha,* where the chin is pressed down on the throat.

There are many different kinds of *mudrās*. Some of them, such as the *mahā mudrā,* are advanced *haṭha yoga* techniques that force the *prāṇa* into the *suṣumnā* and awaken Kundalini. They create pressure, making the Shakti rise and pierce the *chakras*, the subtle energy centers in the central channel. Then, from the *chakras*, the Shakti radiates outward into all the *nāḍīs*, purifying them.

Another variety of *mudrā* is hand gestures, which seal the energy inside the body. They unite the different currents of *prāṇa*, just as rivers converge; then these currents flood the *chakras* with energy. Two of the most common *mudrās* are the *abhaya mudrā,* the gesture of dispelling fear, and the *varada mudrā,* the gesture of granting boons. In the *abhaya mudrā,* the hand is raised with the palm outward. In the *varada mudrā*, the palm is extended outward horizontally and facing up. All the deities in the *chakras* are shown making these two *mudrās*.

Some years ago, a few of us were returning to Gurudev Siddha Peeth late at night following a program in Bombay. A ten-year-old girl who was with us became sleepy and stretched out across our laps in the back seat of the car. Soon she was fast asleep. After a short time, she seemed to enter a state of meditative sleep and began performing classical yogic *mudrās* with the grace of an accomplished dancer. We were amazed at their beauty and perfection.

In another *mudrā,* sometimes the tongue curls back upward against the palate and into the nasal pharynx. This is the *khecharī mudrā,* and it opens the way to the *sahasrāra* and allows divine nectar to be released. Yogis often spend years trying to accomplish this on their own, and may slit the frenum a little at a time to allow the tongue to lengthen. But *khecharī mudrā* may occur as a *kriyā* in Siddha Yoga.

A woman said that during a talk about meditation in an evening program in South Fallsburg, Gurumayi mentioned that when you reach a particular stage of meditation, certain *mudrās* start to occur, including the *khecharī mudrā*. The woman had never heard of that before, and a deep longing arose in her, to the point that she began to weep. A few days later during a chant of

Oṁ Namaḥ Śivāya, she went into a state of bliss. Suddenly, a powerful energy began to shoot up through her body, and her tongue started to move. It curled up and tried to find its way to the back of her mouth. She thought, "This can't be possible," as the force became stronger and stronger. As her tongue rose up against the palate, she said a rain of nectar fell, a sweet liquid that was unimaginably delicious and cool at the same time. As the experience waned, she thought perhaps half an hour had gone by, but when she looked at the clock, she saw that three hours had passed.

The *śambhavi mudrā* is a state of spontaneous *samādhi*, or meditative union with the Absolute, in which the gaze becomes focused within, although the eyes remain half open and appear to be looking outward. A woman said that during an evening program in Gurudev Siddha Peeth, she was watching Gurumayi, who was sitting motionless in *śambhavi mudrā*. At one point the woman started to merge into the *mudrā*. Gurumayi's gaze was like an open door, and the woman walked in. Suddenly, her whole awareness shifted to an experience of the Absolute. There was only That — the source of all creation. It was utterly still and infinite. She described it as becoming the container instead of the contained, becoming the pitcher instead of the water. It permanently altered her life and gave her a tremendous motivation for *sādhana*.

Prāṇāyāma, regulation of the breath, also purifies the *prāṇa* and stabilizes its flow throughout the body. The *prāṇa* and the mind are intimately connected. When the flow of the *prāṇa* is smooth, the mind grows calm and meditation comes easily. In *bhastrikā prāṇāyāma*, the breath is drawn forcefully in and out, like a blacksmith's bellows. *Kumbhaka* is the retention of the breath. These two types of *prāṇāyāma* frequently occur involuntarily as *kriyās* following *śaktipāt*.

A woman said that during her stay in Gurudev Siddha Peeth, she went to the statue of Lord Shiva in the upper gardens and chanted the *Śiva Mahimnah Stotram*. Afterward she fell easily and naturally into meditation. As she listened to the mantra repeating itself inside, her eyes and her awareness were drawn up very powerfully to the top of her head. She watched with fascination as the Shakti played with her breath, drew it in and held it for a long time, then drew it out so thoroughly that her stomach seemed almost to touch her backbone, and then held it out for a long time. She recognized this as *kumbhaka*, a practice which yogis attempt for years and years, and here it was happening to her effortlessly. Her mind would stop, and there would be a space, luminous and infinite, filled with peace.

The texts on *haṭha yoga* say that, ordinarily, the *prāṇa* circulates through the *īḍā* or moon *nāḍī* at night. At that time, the mind and body are lethargic and want to sleep. Yogis are told not to eat when the *prāṇa* is flowing through *īḍā*; the accompanying state of relaxation and coolness makes it difficult to digest food. The *prāṇa* flows through the *piṅgalā* or sun *nāḍī* during the day, and the mind is restless and active. Neither of these conditions is conducive to meditation; the mind is either lethargic or restless. Only when the *prāṇa* enters the *suṣumnā* does the mind turn within and enter a state of meditation. This is why yogic *āsanas* and practices have as their primary aim forcing the *prāṇa* out of *īḍā* and *piṅgalā* and into *suṣumnā*. When the *prāṇa* leaves *īḍā* and *piṅgalā*, they are said to "die"; that is, they are relaxed and devitalized.

The two periods of *saṅdhyā*, the hours of twilight at

dawn and in the evening at dusk, are times of transition when the *prāṇa* is shifting from *īḍā* to *piṅgalā*, or vice versa. They are moments when it is easier for the *prāṇa* to be diverted into the central channel. For this reason, these two periods of twilight are regarded by the scriptures as being particularly auspicious for spiritual practice. When the *prāṇa* enters the *suṣumnā*, Kundalini awakens and rises along with the *prāṇa* through the central channel to the crown of the head, producing the state of *samādhi*.

In an esoteric verse describing this process, a Shaivite scripture says, "If one hopes to assure the perpetual and indivisible blossoming of one's own heart, one must split the center where the sun and moon set."[7]

This happens naturally, with no forcing, after *śaktipāt*. In meditation one can often feel the breathing shift as the *prāṇa* enters the *suṣumnā*. The *prāṇa* may enter subtly, or with a great roar and sensation of heat.

Gurumayi has said:

> When the Shakti is awakened, when both the sun and the moon merge in the royal path, in the *suṣumnā nāḍī*, in the column of light, then you are able to see quite vividly what is right and what is not, what is needed and what is not, what should be done and what should not. There is absolute certainty, absolute confidence because of this experience.[8]

When the *prāṇa* enters the *suṣumnā*, the *suṣumnā* opens up and begins to unfold. The *Pratyabhijñāhridayam* says, "When the central *nāḍī* is unfolded, one acquires the bliss of Consciousness."[9] Baba called the unfolding of the *suṣumnā* "the pilgrimage to liberation." The awakened Kundalini rises through the central channel, purifying it of all the stored past impressions, piercing the *chakras*, loosening the three knots, and leading the seeker ultimately to the bliss of union with the Divine.

These *āsanas*, *bandhas*, *mudrās*, and varieties of *prāṇāyāma* occur as spontaneous *kriyās* when and if necessary after a person receives *śaktipāt*. Not everyone needs them. Baba used to say that *kriyās* are medicine, and he would add, "If you don't have any disease, why should you take medicine?"[10] The Shakti causes them in order to remove particular blockages. When those blocks are removed, the *kriyās* are no longer necessary. And there is no way to predict how long a particular *kriyā* will last. In some seekers they are of short duration, whereas other people may experience them for years. *Kriyās* help purify the body and prepare it to withstand the impact of the Shakti.

A woman who received *śaktipāt* at an Intensive with Baba said that her body suddenly shot up in the full lotus posture and she began to do spontaneous *bhastrikā prāṇāyāma*. She burst into uncontrollable laughter, and then wept deeply. She was worried that she was disturbing everyone else's meditation, but there was very little she could do about it. That afternoon, as she joined the *darśan* line, Baba saw her coming. He got excited and pointed at her, while speaking in Hindi to the people around him. Later on, they told the woman what Baba had said: he had described her experience in minute detail, even though he had left the meditation hall by the time it happened. The woman said she felt a profound sense of oneness with Baba.

In Baba's words:

> What friend can there be like the Shakti-bestowing Guru who, through the inner yogic movements, cleans like a washerman all the limbs and organs of the body...who cleanses its nerves clogged with impurities, and takes away all its disorders...? Working like servants and laborers, he burns up all

> the inner dirt and incinerates it in the fire of yoga until the body is pure gold.[11]

I remember a dream I had several years ago in Gurudev Siddha Peeth. A small group of beautiful women who resembled goddesses approached me and said, "You are going to go through the fire and become gold." They were very kind and explained that there was nothing to worry about, that this was a sacred fire, and to go through it was a great privilege. They began to wrap a wet towel around my hair so it wouldn't burn. Then a second 'I' watched from a few feet away as an intense golden radiance suffused my body. Around my legs and feet I could see flames leaping up, but they were subtler than earthly fire. And soon, my whole body turned to burnished gold. I understood that this was the great work being carried out by Kundalini, the fire of yoga.

Varṇamayī

Just as *kriyāvati* pertains to *haṭha yoga, varṇamayī* pertains to *mantra yoga*. Vocal powers that had previously lain dormant are awakened in a seeker. He may begin to utter words, sentences, and mantras in Sanskrit or other languages that are often completely unknown to him.

As we will see in the next chapter in our discussion of the *chakras*, all mantras, syllables, and sounds are found within us. Each petal of every *chakra* is associated with a particular sound or letter of the Sanskrit alphabet, and these sounds emanate from the *chakras*.

A man who now stays in the South Fallsburg Ashram had extraordinary experiences of a *varṇamayī* awakening. He would feel the Shakti surging up from the base of his spine like a fountain of energy. As it rose through the *suṣumnā* it would begin to vibrate in the *chakras*, and a rapid staccato series of sounds would issue from his mouth like a machine gun. This happened involuntarily, and the sounds were completely foreign to him. One day several Indian men who were sitting near him in the meditation hall told him that he had just recited the entire Sanskrit alphabet in sequence!

He would utter certain syllables which turned out to be *bīja* mantras, or seed letters, also associated with the *chakras*. In addition, he found himself making sounds that resembled the bellowing of a buffalo, the barking of a dog, the roar of a lion, the hissing of a serpent, and various bird calls. This phase lasted a few months; then it never happened to him again.

Another man found that when he sat for meditation after receiving *śaktipāt*, his hands would immediately begin to make involuntary movements. He would touch his stomach, his heart, his throat, and the space between his eyebrows. And as he was touching these places, he began to intone strange sounds — *hriṁ, śriṁ, huṁ*. He had no idea what he was doing, and yet it had a profound effect on his meditation. Two years later while he was leafing through a yogic scripture called the *Mahānirvāṇa Tantra*, he found the explanation: it was a yogic technique known as *nyāsa*, in which the subtle body is infused with *prāṇa*. He had been touching the areas of his body that contained *chakras*, and the sounds he had been making were *bīja* mantras, or Sanskrit seed syllables. He had never studied yoga or Sanskrit, but he was able to execute perfectly an esoteric technique as it was described in a scripture written in India hundreds of years ago.

Varṇamayī also includes literary inspiration and poetic composition. A number of writers have had their writer's block permanently removed by this kind of awakening. One woman went home from her first Intensive and wrote a three-hundred-page novel!

The great German composer Richard Wagner once said that a trance-like condition is the prerequisite of all true creative effort. He felt that he was one with a vibrating force, that it was omniscient, and that he could draw upon it to an extent that was limited only by his own capacity to do so.

Another well-known German composer, Richard Strauss, said that when he was in his most inspired moods, he had compelling visions involving a higher Self. He felt at such moments that he was tapping the source of infinite and eternal energy, from which all things proceed, and which religion calls God.

In other examples of *varṇamayī*, intuitive wisdom arises. A very moving incident took place when we were in Melbourne, Australia, with Baba on his third world tour. Baba had just given an Intensive and had retired to his quarters for the evening. I was doing some work in his Namaste Room, where Baba received people, across the hall. Suddenly, there was a knock on the door, which was Baba's private entrance and was reserved for his use. I went to answer it and found a lovely little Catholic nun. "Is Swami Muktananda here?" she asked sweetly. I explained to her that Baba had already gone in for the evening and was not meeting anyone. She looked crestfallen and said, "Oh please, I've driven seventy miles from the convent to come here, and I don't want to go back without seeing him." I went to find Baba's attendant, Swami Sevananda, and told him the story. Sevananda disappeared into Baba's room.

A few minutes later, Baba came out and told me to show her into his Namaste Room. He sat down in his chair and, with great tenderness, motioned for her to come close to him. The little nun burst into tears and fell at his feet. She explained that she had seen Baba's face on the TV news, and something had happened to her. She began to go into spontaneous meditation and was having a direct experience of the scriptural truths she had studied in her catechism as a young girl. Until now, she had understood them only intellectually. At last, she realized the essence of what they were saying. Baba wiped away her tears and stroked her cheeks with tremendous love. *"Bahut accha!"* he exclaimed softly. "Very good!"

For another woman, Kundalini manifested as wisdom and as the guidance of a strong inner voice. She described it as the voice of God, awakened within her. After this had gone on for some time, she approached a Siddha Yoga swami and told him what she was hearing within. "That's the *Bhagavad Gītā!*" he said. "It is?" she replied. So she looked in the *Bhagavad Gītā,* and it was all there. Then one night, during an evening program in South Fallsburg, someone began to read from Baba's new book, *Reflections of the Self,* and an astonishing thing began to happen. The voice within her would recite the lines before the speaker had a chance to say them. Always a phrase or two ahead of him, it spoke words that no one had ever heard before.

A word of caution is due here. Before acting on the prompting of an inner voice, we must ask ourselves, "Is this really the voice of the higher Self, or is it the voice of the mind, the voice of desire, the voice of the ego?" To obey an inner voice unquestioningly is often to act out of delusion. We have to use great discrimination and measure the content against the highest teachings of the scriptures. Baba often remarked that the inner voice can be unreliable until a person is fully realized.

Saint Teresa of Avila once wrote about the insight that arises from within:

> When in this state of quiet, I, who understand hardly anything that I recite in Latin, particularly in the psalter, have not only been able to understand the text as though it were in Spanish, but have even found to my delight that I can penetrate the meaning of the Spanish.[12]

And she described the intellectual aspect of enlightenment, saying that it was as if a person who was not able to read, and who had never studied, were suddenly to find himself in possession of all the data accumulated by science.

Kalāvati

In *kalāvati*, the awakened Kundalini purifies all the thirty-six *tattvas*, the gross and subtle principles of which the various bodies and sheaths are composed. (See Appendix.) As each of the principles is purified, the seeker automatically detaches himself from it and ceases to identify with it. Finally, the Self alone remains, and he realizes his true identity as Shiva, the Absolute.

In Siddha Yoga, this process may be carried out spontaneously by the awakened Kundalini Shakti, but it can also be used as a practice or a technique of *sādhana*. For example, the *Vijñāna Bhairava* says: "If the yogi contemplates that the progressively subtler principles of his body or of the world are being absorbed into their own respective causes, then the supreme Goddess is finally revealed."[13]

This refers to the technique of *vyāpti*, or fusion, whereby the gross *tattvas* are reabsorbed into the subtler ones. The material elements are to be contemplated as being absorbed into the subtle elements (sound, touch, form, taste, and smell), the subtle elements into the mind and the other psychic instruments, and so on, until everything is finally reabsorbed into the Self.

As we have already seen, the negative qualities and the passions are associated with the lower areas of the *suṣumnā*. As the awakened Kundalini purifies us, these lower qualities tend to disappear and to be replaced by the higher qualities in the upper regions of the central channel. This also pertains to *kalāvati*, the absorption of the gross into the subtle and more refined. The temptations of the ancient Desert Fathers, their visions of demons and vipers, are a graphic example of this process of inner transformation. And the representation of Saint George slaying the dragon illustrates the triumph of the higher nature over the lower.

The awakened Shakti purifies the different senses. Baba said, "On Her journey to the *sahasrāra*, Kundalini passes through all the sense organs, purifying them and investing them with new powers. As long as the *chakras* of the sense organs are not purified, the senses work in an ordinary manner, but when they are purified, they acquire divine powers and even the physical senses become sharpened and refined."[14] The eyes gain the power of seeing even distant objects, the ears can hear the inner music, and divine fragrances and nectar are released.

Experiences of *kalāvati* can be of many varieties. A few years ago we made a pilgrimage to Baba Muktananda's meditation hut at Suki, near the town of Yeola in Maharashtra, India. This is a tiny hut shaded by two large mango trees next to a sugarcane field, where Baba performed intense austerities and spiritual practices after he received *śaktipāt* from his Guru, Bhagawan Nityananda. The force of the Shakti is very intense in that hut, and it permeates the surrounding area as well. I sat down beside the hut and rested against one of the walls, intending to meditate for a while. I didn't even have time to close my eyes — a red glow spread out before me, then a brilliant white circle of light appeared within it. These were replaced by an intensely black circle, smaller in size, and finally the shimmering Blue Pearl flashed before me.

These were the lights associated with the four bodies that Baba describes in his spiritual autobiography, *Play of Consciousness.* The red aura corresponds to the physical body, the white light to the subtle body, the black light to the causal body, and the Blue Pearl to the supracausal body. Each one progressively dissolves into its subtle cause.

Another variety of *kalāvati* experience is a vision of the dissolution of all forms into light. During one of Gurumayi's tours in California, a woman approached her in the *darśan* line and said, "I'm so filled with longing for God that I can't sleep. I wake up every hour all night long. I don't know what to do." Gurumayi took her hand, pulled her close, and looked into her eyes. The woman said, "I felt her gaze enter the deepest part of my being. I opened myself to her and let her in. The hall disappeared; the music and the people were gone. Then I vanished and so did she, and there was nothing but light. Then something shifted, and the world came back." The woman returned to her seat and wept for the remainder of *darśan*. Her deepest longing had been fulfilled.

Vedhamayī

In *vedhamayī*, one experiences the piercing of the *chakras*. This may take a variety of forms — a sensation of intense pressure or vibration at the different centers, or visions of the *chakras* opening. In meditation, one woman saw herself as a beautiful vine growing on the side of a house. The vine had seven flowers, whose heads were hanging downward. Then a powerful energy began to rise up the vine. Each time it reached a flower, the flower would lift its head, open, and reveal the most extraordinary interior. They were of different colors — red, yellow, white, and purple. When the energy rose to the topmost flower, the largest of all, it lifted its head to reveal a magnificent thousand-petaled lotus, radiating golden light.

Another woman said that one day Baba Muktananda hit her on the back several times very hard when she went up to him in the *darśan* line. She went to her room to lie down, and she felt tremendous warmth suffusing her spinal column. A friend told her that her spine was beet red and very hot to the touch. A few hours later the woman had a vision. She saw herself inside a firehouse, and there was a fireman's pole extending up through seven stories. At the bottom there were two snakes that began winding their way up. The snakes pushed through each story until they finally reached the top of the pole.

One of the most significant centers is the *anāhata chakra* at the heart. Baba Muktananda says: "When Kundalini reaches this level, the heart opens, and waves upon waves of bliss keep arising within. There is a beautiful light in the heart, which one sees in meditation. Moreover, there is a center of pure knowledge there, and when Kundalini begins to work in the heart, knowledge arises in you spontaneously. Different powers such as clairaudience, clairvoyance, and the power of healing come automatically."[15]

In many instances of *śaktipāt*, there is a dramatic opening of the heart and one is overcome by powerful waves of divine love, a love that is pure and uncontaminated by the passions of the lower centers. Baba also said that when the heart opens, one begins to experience the different inner worlds. These can be truly astonishing — cities of light, of gold, of crystal, where the inner experience is one of ecstasy, or lower realms inhabited by curious beings half human and half animal.

A woman who was staying in Gurudev Siddha Peeth said that one day she was lying in bed looking at a photograph of Gurumayi. All of a sudden a blue light, a star, appeared, and it grew bigger and bigger. It came toward her and enveloped her. The next thing she knew, she was flying through the air at a speed of thousands of miles an hour. Suddenly, she landed in a realm that was entirely blue. She knew there were objects there, but she could not distinguish them. All she could see was blue light. Then a blue being approached her and said, "This is where you will come one day. But first you must repeat this mantra." He gave her a mantra, which she began to repeat. As she did this, the blue star once again carried her back to her bed at the same incredible rate of speed. But before she knew what was happening, the blue star returned and took her away again, this time even faster. She landed in the same place, and the blue being appeared once more. He said, "I told you to repeat the mantra." So she began repeating it very intensely, over and over. Her experience in that world was one of ecstasy, she said, but she had the distinct sense that she was not yet strong enough to contain the energy there, which was overwhelming. A moment later, she went flying back through the cosmos and landed on her bed, with the mantra repeating itself inside her.

As Kundalini rises up to the higher centers, a seeker experiences visions of light in various forms, such as the moon, the sun, stars, fire, lightning, and flame. Much of the scriptural literature on Kundalini has to do with Her manifestation in the form of inner light.

Jnaneshwar Maharaj says: "She is like a ring of lightning, folds of flaming fire, or a bar of pure gold.... When She is awakened, She breaks Her bonds like a star shooting through space, like the sun falling from its place in the sky, or a point of light bursting forth like a sprouting seed."[16]

Gurumayi once said:

> Have you ever seen the fireworks that are called sparklers? They take one that is already lit to light one that is unlit, and then use the newly lit one to light another. And then one more, one more, one more. Then you have all these stars!
>
> There are *chakras*, spiritual centers, within the subtle system which are described as lotuses. When you repeat the mantra, you experience the stars in each of these centers. The mantra takes you from one star to another, from the second to the third, from the third to the fourth. And in this way, the entire body is illumined with the light of Consciousness; the entire body radiates light.
>
> Many people want to know how they can create a body of light so that they can move very easily. For this, repeat the mantra. It will take you from one star to the next until it reaches the top of the head, which is called the *sahasrāra*. When all those stars finally hit that one big light, there is nothing but light![17]

The inner divine sounds, or *nāda*, are also associated with *vedhamayī*. They are categorized into ten varieties: the humming of bees, the roar of the ocean, the ringing of bells, the sound of the conch, the *vīnā* (a stringed instrument), cymbals, the flute, the *mridaṅg* (a drum), the kettledrum, and the sound of thunder. Most of these originate in the heart *chakra*, but the *megha nāda*, thunder, resounds in the *sahasrāra*. The mind becomes overpowered, loses consciousness, merges into the sound or light, and ultimately into the Self. For this reason, *vedhamayī* also pertains to *laya yoga*.

Siddha Yoga is called *mahā yoga,* the great yoga, because it encompasses all these other independent yogas. In the words of Baba Muktananda: "Just as a seed contains a whole tree in potential form, Kundalini contains all the different forms of yoga, and when She is awakened through the grace of the Guru, She makes all yogas take place within you spontaneously.... You don't have to make any effort to practice them; they come to you on their own."[18]

Notes to Chapter 6

1 Swami Muktananda, *Kundalini, The Secret of Life,* 2d edition (New York: SYDA Foundation, 1980), p. 22.

2 Swami Vishnu Tirtha Maharaj, *Śaktipāt — Kundalini Mahayoga* (Sanskrit/Hindi edition; Devas, Madhya Pradesh: Shri Sadhan Granthamala Prakashan Samiti Narayana Kuti, Sannyas Ashram) 4:30-31.

3 *Parātriṁśika Vivaraṇa.*

4 Swami Muktananda, "A Million Times Brighter Than the Sun," *Darshan* magazine 41/42 (1990), p. 60.

5 *Rig Veda* 1:8:3.

6 *Śaktipāt — Kundalini Mahayoga,* 2:16.
See also, by the same author, *Devātma Shakti* (1968 edition; Rishikesh, India: Muni Ki Rati, 1948), pp. 79-100.

7 *Mahārthamañjarī* 55.

8 *Darshan* magazine 41/42, p. 79.

9 *Pratyabhijñāhridayam* 17.

10 Swami Muktananda, *From the Finite to the Infinite* (New York: SYDA Foundation, 1989), vol 1, p. 84.

11 Swami Muktananda, *Play of Consciousness,* translated by Swami Chidvilasananda (New York: SYDA Foundation, 1974), p. 22.

12 *The Life of Teresa of Jesus,* translated and edited by E. Allison Peers (Garden City, New York: Image Books, 1960), p. 158.

13 *Vijñāna Bhairava* dharana 31.

14 *Kundalini,The Secret of Life,* p. 38.

15 Ibid., p. 32.

16 *Jnaneshwar's Gītā,* rendered by Swami Kripananda (Albany: State University of New York Press, 1989) 6:224, 226.

17 Swami Chidvilasananda, "Creating a Body of Light," *Darshan* magazine 41/42 (1990), p. 168.

18 *Kundalini,The Secret of Life,* p. 18.

The deities residing in the chakras tremble when the prāṇa moves through the suṣumnā, and the great Goddess Kundalini is absorbed in Mount Kailāsa in the sahasrāra.

— *Śiva Saṁhitā* 4:26

CHAPTER 7

THE CHAKRAS:

Lotuses of Light

The poet-saint Kabir said:

Within this earthen vessel are bowers and groves,
And within it is the Creator.
Within this vessel are the seven oceans
and the unnumbered stars.
The touchstone and the jewel appraiser are within;
And within this vessel the Eternal soundeth,
and the spring wells up.
Kabir says:
Listen to me, my friend!
My beloved Lord is within.[1]

Kabir had discovered through his own direct personal experience the scriptural truth that all the principles of creation exist right within us. Our bodies and the universe are composed of the same principles. For this reason, the scriptures talk about the identity of the *brahmāṇḍa*, the macrocosm, and the *piṇḍāṇḍa*, the microcosm or human body.

We have already seen that, just as the Absolute descends through its manifestations from the subtle to the gross in the outer world, it does the same thing in our own bodies. On the individual level, the Supreme descends from the *sahasrāra* at the crown of the head and manifests as the various creative principles, or *tattvas*, from the subtle to the gross, in the six *chakras* within the *suṣumnā nāḍī*. Each *tattva* has its own center of activity within the body, from which energy is radiated into the system. These centers are called *chakras*, and they are junction points where *nāḍīs* converge like the spokes of a wheel inside the *suṣumnā*. The *prāṇa* is diffused from the *chakras* throughout the entire system through the complex web of *nāḍīs*.

These subtle centers vitalize and control the various organs, nerves, and plexi of the physical body in the regions surrounding each *chakra*. The *chakras* are extremely subtle centers of vital energy. The nerve plexi and organs which correspond to them in the physical body are built up by their coarsened vibrations. Because the *chakras* and the *nāḍīs* belong to the subtle body, they cannot be seen with the physical eyes. They exist only as long as the body is alive and disappear when the life force leaves the body.

One morning while I was sitting for meditation, I suddenly felt all the vitality in my body withdraw itself from my limbs and gather in the center of my body. It rose up through the central channel and exited through the crown of my head, taking my full awareness intact along with it. I felt that I was formless consciousness, completely independent of my physical body, which I could observe from a few feet away. There was nothing frightening about it — I was still "me" as I knew myself, but without a body. Then, just as suddenly, I returned to my body, reentering it through the crown of the head. As the vital force descended through the *suṣumnā*, it shot out into all my limbs through an infinite number of tiny channels, revitalizing them once more. The subtle body again interpenetrated and enlivened the physical body. I now understood what happens at the moment of physical death, and that what we truly are in essence survives the death of the body without any break in consciousness. It answered the questions I had had for years regarding the survival of the soul after death.

The *chakras* are often referred to as lotuses with varying numbers of petals. The petals are formed by the configurations of the *nāḍīs*, which surround and pass through the *chakras*. Each *nāḍī* has its own particular rate of vibration, and each vibrational level produces a specific sound. The sound produced by the vibrations of the *nāḍīs* is represented by the corresponding Sanskrit letters, which appear on the petals of the lotuses.

Because each letter of the Sanskrit alphabet is a separate power and a particular aspect of God, it is considered a *devatā*, or deity. The letters on the petals are therefore termed the surrounding deities of the principal deity or governor of the *chakra*, and a *chakra* has as many of these subsidiary deities as it has petals.

The sages discovered that, by repeating these syllables, they could affect the corresponding *nāḍīs* and *chakras* and could bring about highly predictable results. In this way, they learned how to develop certain *siddhis*, or supernormal powers, such as the ability to levitate, to reduce the body to the size of an atom, to expand it to any size, and so on. Baba strongly discouraged people from trying to cultivate supernormal powers. They are obvious ego traps; they distract us from our highest purpose and they siphon off our energy at lower levels. He used to say that the only *siddhi* worth attaining was the *mahā* or great *siddhi*, the state of absorption in God.

Far more important, the sages also discovered particular Sanskrit syllables, or combinations of syllables (among which are *Rāma*, *Krişṇa*, and *Namaḥ Śivāya*), which create within the central channel, the *suṣumnā nāḍī*, powerful vibrations capable of awakening Kundalini. Since Kundalini awakening eventually culminates in God-realization, these syllables came to be called the Names of God.[2]

With regard to the *siddhis*, an Indian scholar says:

> We can meet with several persons every day elbowing us in the streets or bazaars who in all sincerity attempted to reach the highest plane of bliss, but fell victim on the way to the illusions of the psychic world, and stopped at one or the other of the six *chakras*. They are of varying degrees of attainment and are seen to possess some power which is not found even in the best intellectuals of the ordinary run of mankind. That this school of practical psychology was working very well in India at one time is evident from these living instances (not to speak of the numberless treatises on the subject) of men roaming about in all parts of the country.[3]

Each *chakra*, with the exception of the *sahasrāra*, has a *bīja* mantra, or seed letter, which represents the subtle sound produced by the vibration of the forces of that particular *chakra*. The seed letter expresses the essential nature of the *chakra*. As we have seen, the five lower *chakras* are the bodily centers for the *tattvas* of the five material elements: earth, water, fire, air, and ether. Each *chakra* is represented by the seed letter which corresponds to its specific element. The sixth *chakra*, *ājñā*, is represented by the sacred syllable *Oṁ*. The seed letters are the audible forms of the principles of creation, and they are the "natural name" of the element associated with that *chakra*. The element springs from its seed mantra, or natural name, and also eventually reenters it. If a person utters with creative force the natural name of anything, he brings that thing into existence.

For instance, *raṁ* is the seed mantra or natural name of fire in the *maṇipūra chakra* at the navel. So the mantra *raṁ* is the sound audible to the physical ears of the forces constituting fire. The same thing is true of the other seed mantras in the other *chakras*: *laṁ* in *mūlādhāra* at the base of the spine — earth; *vaṁ* in *svādhiṣṭhāna* in the sacral area — water; *yaṁ* in *anāhata* at the heart — air; and *haṁ* in *viśuddha* at the throat — ether. However, merely repeating *raṁ* will not produce fire. The mantra has to be awakened and made *chaitanya*, or conscious, for it to work. Otherwise, the scriptures explain, one repeats it at the layer of the outer husk; it must be enlivened at its core, and then repeated with creative force.

The elements of the *chakras* are also associated with the various senses and their corresponding *tattvas*: the powers of sense perception (smell, taste, sight, touch, and hearing), the powers of action (locomotion, grasping or handling, excretion, reproduction and sexual enjoyment, and speaking), and the subtle elements of perception (which, when they reach the gross level of manifestation, will form the objects of the senses — odor, taste, form and color, touch, and sound).

When a seeker practices Kundalini yoga without the grace of a Siddha Guru, he must propitiate each of the deities residing in each of the *chakras*. The Tantras describe the specific forms of worship required by each of the hundreds of deities before Kundalini can rise — a very time-consuming process indeed!*

The *Ṣaṭ Chakra Nirūpaṇa* ("An Investigation of the Six

* For instance, a particular meditation on Dakini says: "Meditate on her, the red, the red-eyed Dakini, in the *mūlādhāra chakra*, who strikes terror into the hearts of bound souls, who holds in her two right hands a spear and a staff surmounted by a skull, and in her two left hands a sword and a cup. She is fierce of temper and shows her ferocious teeth. She crushes the whole host of enemies. She is plump of body and is fond of rice pudding. It is thus that she should be meditated upon by those who desire immortality."[4]

Chakras") is a Sanskrit text composed in the sixteenth century by the great Master Purnananda Swami. The commentary, written by Kalicharana, begins with these words: "He alone who has become acquainted with the wealth of the six lotuses by *mahā yoga* is able to explain the inner principles thereof. Not even the most excellent among the wise, nor the oldest in experience, is able, without the mercy of the Guru, to explain the inner principles relating to the six *chakras*."[5]

The six principal deities of the *chakras*, in ascending order, are: Brahma, Vishnu, Rudra, Isha, Sadashiva, and Shambhu. They govern the six corresponding planes or realms: *bhūrloka* (the earth), *bhūvarloka* (the plane of the ancestors), *svarloka* (the celestial realm), and *maharloka, janaloka,* and *tapaloka,* which are planes of highly evolved beings. The *sahasrāra* corresponds to *satyaloka,* the realm of pure Consciousness, the abode of supreme Shiva. In this way, the *chakras* are related to the various planes of the macrocosm, which may be experienced in meditation as Kundalini pierces the *chakras* corresponding to them.

Along with their deities, the *chakras* have their own particular Shaktis, which represent the various *dhātus,* or bodily substances: skin, blood, flesh, fat, bone, and marrow. These Shaktis are sometimes called the Queens of the *chakras* or their doorkeepers.

The petals of the lotuses hang downward except when Kundalini passes through them. As the *nāḍīs* are filled with the radiant Shakti, the lotuses appear to turn upward and bloom with light.

A number of scriptures in the Kundalini tradition[6] list various qualities that are associated with the different *chakras*. They explain that there exists a connection between the particular qualities and the operation of the energies of the *chakra* to which the qualities are assigned. They also state that those qualities tend to disappear when Kundalini rises through the corresponding *chakra*. In this way, the undesirable negative qualities associated with the lower *chakras* vanish in a person who raises Kundalini above them. As one reaches the higher centers, the qualities become increasingly good.

There are three "male" Shiva *liṅgams*, symbols of Shiva, one located in the *mūlādhāra chakra* at the base of the spine, one in the *anāhata chakra* at the heart, and the third in the *ājñā chakra* at the space between the eyebrows. They are set in "female" (apex down) triangles, which are seats of Shakti. These are the locations of the three *granthis*, or knots, where the force of *māyā* is said to be exceptionally strong.

Mūlādhāra Chakra

The *mūlādhāra chakra* lies at the root of the *suṣumnā nāḍī* at the base of the spine, where Kundalini lies dormant. *Mūla* means "root," and *adhāra* is "support." The three principal *nāḍīs* — *īḍā*, *piṅgalā*, and *suṣumnā* — are also known as Ganga, Yamuna, and Saraswati, respectively, named after three sacred rivers of India. Because they converge here at the *mūlādhāra chakra*, this place is called *yukta-triveṇi*. The Sanskrit word *triveṇi* means the place of confluence of these three rivers, and *yukta* means "yoked or joined"; it can also mean "auspicious."

The sun, moon, and fire are frequent images in the scriptures on Kundalini, because these are the most common forms the Great Light takes when it descends into the realm of matter. We are all very familiar with these outer manifestations of light, but we are not so well acquainted with their inner counterparts. Usually, these three forms of light are grouped according to their degree of subtlety. Each one is associated with one of the three *guṇas*, the basic qualities of nature that determine the inherent characteristics of all created things. Fire is the grossest of the three and is associated with *tamo guṇa*, the impure quality. The sun is subtler and represents *rajo guṇa*, which is both pure and impure. The moon, which is cooling and white, is regarded as the subtlest form of light and is connected with *sattva guṇa*, the quality of goodness and purity.

The *īḍā nāḍī* on the left of the *suṣumnā* is called the moon *nāḍī*. It is cooling and of a pale silvery color. *Piṅgalā*, on the right, is the sun *nāḍī*. It is heating and has the luster of the filaments of the pomegranate flower. The *suṣumnā* is the central channel and is fiery. The *suṣumnā* is actually composed of a number of layers or concentric circles, which are also considered *nāḍīs*. The outermost layer is the *suṣumnā*, representing fire and *tamo guṇa*. Within it is the *vajra nāḍī*, associated with the sun and *rajo guṇa*, and within that is the *chitriṇī nāḍī*, related to the moon and *sattva guṇa*. *Chitriṇī* is said to be as subtle as a spider's thread. The space within *chitriṇī* is called the *brahmā nāḍī*, the "channel of the Absolute," and it is the pathway of the awakened Kundalini.

All the *nāḍīs* originate in the *kāṇḍa*, a Sanskrit word meaning "bulb." It is located between the anus and the reproductive organ and is shaped like a bird's egg.

The *mūlādhāra chakra* has four petals, whose qualities are four forms of bliss, since this center is the "source of a massive pleasurable sensation." On these petals, which are crimson, are the golden letters *vaṁ, śaṁ, ṣaṁ,* and *saṁ.* The letters begin at the top and go in a clockwise direction around the petals.

This is the center of the densest *tattva*, earth, to which the Tantras assign the color yellow. The square is the *maṇḍala*, geometric form, of the earth principle, and it is surrounded by eight spears directed toward the eight points of the compass.

The seed letter of earth is *laṁ*, which is shown seated on the elephant Airavata, the vehicle of Indra, the Vedic lord of the celestial beings. The elephant symbolizes the strength and solidity of the earth. The seed letters are personified in order to aid in their visualization. They are represented with various numbers of arms and are mounted on vehicles. Earth has the property of cohesion and stimulates the sense of smell, so the power of smelling *(ghrāṇendriya)* is associated with this center, along with smell-as-such *(gandha tanmātra)*, and the power of locomotion *(pādendriya)*.[7]

The deity of this *chakra* is the creator, Brahma, with four faces, so creativity is also connected with this center. Many of the scriptures cite this *chakra* as the location of *parā*, the supreme or subtlest state of sound which, as vibration, gives rise to the entire universe.

The deities of all the *chakras* actually reside in the *bindu*, or dot, above the seed letter, but for want of space, they have been pictured outside. Along with the *devatā* there is always a *devī*, in this case the Shakti Dakini, representing the *dhātu* of skin. She serves as the keeper of the door, the *brahmā-dvara*, or entrance to the *suṣumnā*. All of the *devatās* and *devīs* are shown making the gestures of dispelling fear *(abhaya mudrā)* and granting boons *(varada mudrā)*.

In the center of the *chakra* there is the lightning-like *traipura* triangle, the seat of Shakti, within which is set the *svayaṁbhu liṅgam*. The Sanskrit word *svayaṁbhu* means "self-originated" or "self-existent," and it is one of the names of Brahma. This *liṅgam* is described as beautiful like molten gold and of the shape and color of a new leaf. This is the location of the *Brahmā granthi*, the first of the three knots that must be severed. Sometimes a sensation of pulling or contraction takes place in this region, and one may feel the *prāṇa* leaving the *īḍā* and *piṅgalā nāḍīs* and entering the *suṣumnā*.

Around the *liṅgam* the sleeping Kundalini is coiled three and a half times, covering with Her mouth the entrance to the *suṣumnā*. *The Ṣaṭ Chakra Nirūpaṇa* describes Her as follows:

> Over the *liṅgam* shines the sleeping Kundalini, fine as the fiber of the lotus stalk. She is the world-bewilderer, gently covering the mouth of the *brahmā-dvara* with Her own. Like the spiral of the conch shell, Her shining snake-like form goes three and a half times around Shiva; and Her luster is like that of a strong flash of young lightning. Her sweet murmur is like the indistinct hum of swarms of love-mad bees. She produces melodious poetry and all other compositions in prose or verse in Sanskrit and other languages. It is She who maintains all the beings in the world by means of the inhalation and exhalation, and shines in the cavity of the root lotus like a chain of brilliant lights.[8]

One day in a meditation vision, a woman found herself struggling on her hands and knees down through a narrow cavern. At the bottom she discovered a small serpent, coiled in a prism of water, surrounded by brilliant light. The woman knew that the serpent had been patiently waiting for her to come and kneel at her shrine. As she knelt, the serpent became vast and bit her; then the woman discovered that she had within her all power and all wisdom.

Gurumayi once said that people speak of Kundalini as moving in a column from the base of the spine to the crown of the head, and they try to grasp Her in this way. But in the realm of Kundalini, nothing is dense. All

Her colors are translucent.

Gurumayi said:

> Picture Kundalini as a rainbow. She softly glistens in the form of an arch, across the inner sky. A rainbow is not fixed. It arches across the sky like a bow, and yet it is more than a bow or an arch. It is the visible half of a vast circle. The other half is obscured by the earth. Think of the movement of the awakened Kundalini in this way. She is a vast spinning circle of brilliant colors. She cannot be confined. Reality in the world of Kundalini is dazzling.[9]

Svādhiṣṭhāna Chakra

This is the second *chakra*, in ascending order, and is the spinal center of the region at the root of the reproductive organ. Its name means "own abode" of the Shakti. It is a vermilion lotus of six petals, which bear the lightning-colored letters *baṁ, bhaṁ, maṁ, yaṁ, raṁ,* and *laṁ*.

This is the center of the water *tattva*, which is represented by a white inner lotus of eight petals with a crescent moon, the *maṇḍala* of the water principle, in the center. This is the white region of Varuna, the Vedic god of the sea. The seed letter of water is *vaṁ,* stainless and white as the autumnal moon, which is represented as seated on its vehicle, a white *makara*. The *makara* is an animal similar to an alligator, which is the emblem of the waters and the vehicle of Varuna.

Water stimulates the sense of taste, so the power of tasting *(rasanendriya)* is connected with this *chakra*, along with taste-as-such *(rasa tanmātra)*, and the power of grasping or handling *(hastendriya)*.

In the *bindu* of *vaṁ* is Vishnu, the deity of the *chakra*, seated on his vehicle, Garuda, the king of the birds. The *devī* is the Shakti Rakini, representing the bodily substance of blood, whose mind is exalted with the drinking of ambrosia, the nectar which flows from the *sahasrāra*. She is exalted with the divine energy that infuses her. She is described as being of furious aspect. Her three eyes are red, and her teeth show fiercely.

The *svādhiṣṭhāna chakra* is concerned with the excitation of sexual feelings and is associated with the qualities of credulity, suspicion, disdain, delusion, false knowledge, and pitilessness. Each of the six petals of the lotus is associated with one of these particular *vrittis*, or qualities.

When Kundalini yoga is practiced without the grace of a Siddha Guru, it involves intense concentration on the individual *chakras*. This is why so much emphasis is placed on the seeker's purity, self-control, and benevolence. If a seeker has these qualities, it is possible that concentration on the lower centers associated with the passions may quiet them instead of rousing them. On the other hand, if an individual lacks these qualities, his practice may bring about undesirable results.[10]

Gurumayi once said:

> When Kundalini rises to this *chakra* and begins to purify it, all sorts of things come up. If a seeker is upheld and sustained by the practices of yoga, then these negative qualities will be purified gradually and expelled from his system. When you truly believe in the Guru's grace, when you genuinely love and honor Kundalini, then the awakened energy stays under control.
>
> Throughout the ages, the knowers of the Truth have warned seekers not to try to awaken Kundalini on their own. They have pointed out the risks of forcing Kundalini awake through strenuous austerities or radical forms of *prāṇāyāma*. The grace of an enlightened Master is crucial.

> Heaven and hell are in the body. When you get caught up in the six enemies, you are living in hell. But this region only poses a problem for those who want to keep indulging in it. If you care for the Shakti, if you honor and conserve it, then the lotus of *svādhiṣṭhāna* won't trap you. You can live in this very body as if it were heaven.[11]

The scriptures say that a person who successfully meditates on this lotus is freed from the enemies of man, the six passions. Moreover, "He becomes a lord among yogis and is like the sun, illumining the dense darkness of ignorance."[12]

Maṇipūra Chakra

Maṇipūra is the third *chakra*, in ascending order, and is located within the *suṣumnā* at the level of the navel. It is called *maṇipūra* because it is as lustrous as a gem (*maṇi*). It owes its radiance to the fact that it is the center of the fire *tattva*. This lotus is described as having the color of heavy-laden rain clouds; and it has ten petals on which are the letters *ḍaṁ, ḍhaṁ, ṇaṁ, taṁ, thaṁ, daṁ, dhaṁ, naṁ, paṁ,* and *phaṁ.*

The *maṇḍala* of the red region of fire is the triangle, located in the center of the lotus. There is an auspicious swastika on each of its three sides, representing eternality. The seed letter of fire is *raṁ,* as radiant as the rising sun, which is represented as seated on a ram. The ram is the vehicle of Agni, the Vedic lord of fire.

The element of fire has the properties of expansion, producing heat, and stimulating the sight-sense of color and form, so the power of seeing (*chakṣurindriya*) and color-as-such (*rūpa tanmātra*) are associated with this center, as well as the power of excretion (*payvindriya*).

The deity of this *chakra* is Rudra, whose function is the

dissolution of the world. Just as fire consumes everything, so Rudra dissolves everything within himself. He is red but appears to be white because of the ashes he smears on his body. The *devī* of this center is the Shakti Lakini, representing flesh. Like all the other *devīs,* her mind is exalted from drinking the nectar that flows through the *suṣumnā* from the *sahasrāra*. It is said that concentration on this center may satisfy the appetites of this *devī*.

The qualities associated with the petals of this lotus are shame, treachery, jealousy, desire, inertia, sadness, worldliness, ignorance, aversion, and fear. The qualities of this lower center are all still negative. Not until we reach the heart *chakra* do we find a mixture of both positive and negative traits. However, if a yogi successfully meditates on this navel lotus, he acquires the power to destroy and create the world.[13]

Gurumayi once said:

> Allow the awakened Kundalini to convert your lower tendencies into virtues. It is not enough to have a sublime experience in meditation, if all you do is say, "Wow!" — and then go on with your life in a way that contradicts the purity of that experience. With the grace of the awakened Kundalini, you can meditate on these lower *chakras* and transform their qualities into virtues. This is how the darkness of *māyā* is destroyed.[14]

So at *maṇipūra*, for instance, shame can be transformed into honor, treachery into loyalty, sadness into joy, and so on. One of the qualities that is purified at this *chakra* is fear. One man, shortly after he received *śaktipāt*, found that the region around his navel began to vibrate with great intensity. Then he experienced spontaneous *bhastrikā prāṇāyāma*, the bellows breathing. Suddenly, a ball of white light entered his navel and

Mūlādhāra Chakra

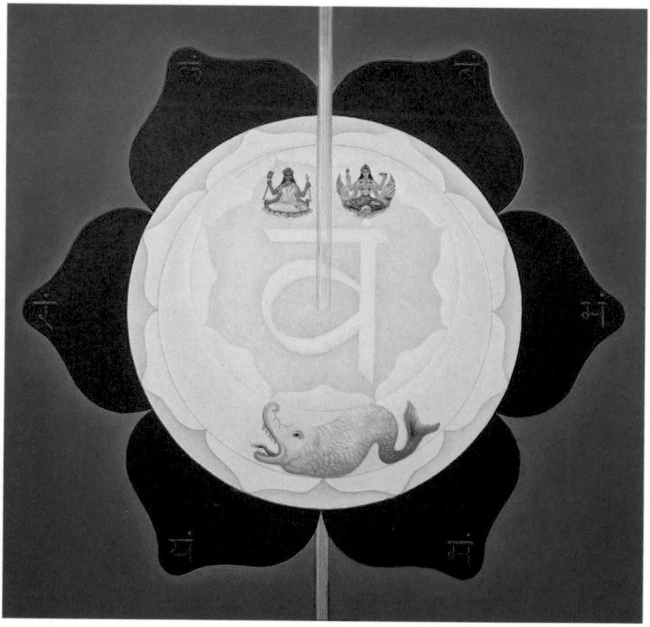

Svādhiṣṭhāna Chakra

Maṇipūra Chakra

Anāhata Chakra

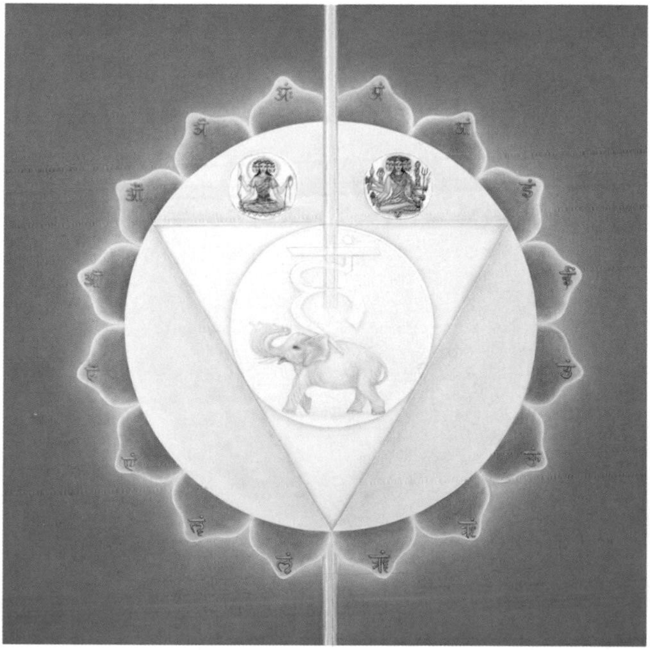

Viśuddha Chakra

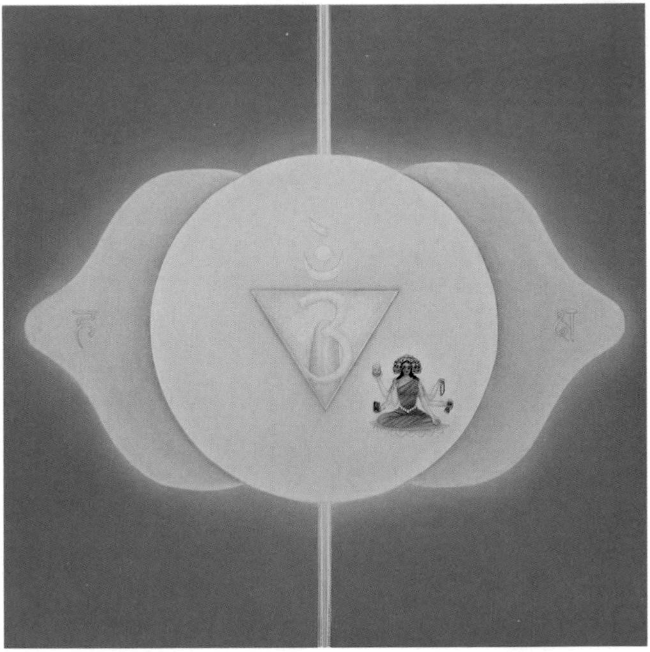

Ājñā Chakra

Sahasrāra

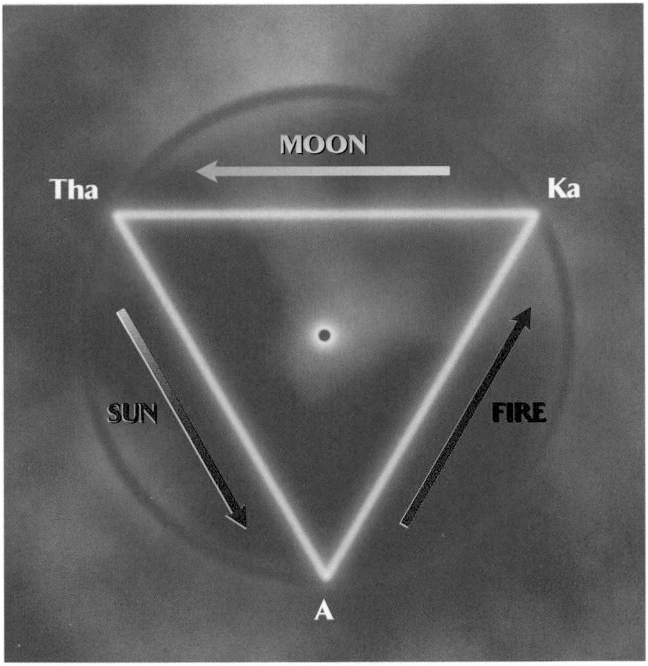

A-ka-tha triangle

exploded. He began to feel completely grounded, and his mind became still. He was filled with a sense of power and fearlessness. Over the next few days the experience remained with him, and he could feel the Shakti emanating from the center at his navel and streaming into his arms and legs.

The element of fire in the *maṇipūra chakra* can be experienced in several different ways. When this center is not purified, its fire can scorch us in craving and desire for worldly pleasure. But when the Kundalini Shakti is awakened and this *chakra* is being purified, that fire becomes the fire of purification in which all our negative qualities are burned. The scriptures say that we can actually offer these qualities to the divine fire within us:

> Into the Fire of Consciousness in the *maṇipūra chakra*,
> kindled with knowledge,
> I offer the actions of the senses,
> with the mind as sacrificial ladle, *svāhā!*
> I offer the senses into the Fire of the Self,
> fueled by righteousness and unrighteousness
> as the clarified butter,
> with the mind as the ladle,
> held by the handle that is the path of *suṣumnā*, *svāhā!*
> I offer all actions, both good and evil,
> into the all-pervading Fire, fed by Time.
> The two hands with which
> I hold the ladle are Shiva and Shakti.
> I offer as oblation this universe of thirty-six principles,
> into the Fire of Consciousness, which even
> without fuel, is constantly burning within.
> Though it is obscured by the darkness of *māyā*,
> it emits rays of wondrous purifying light, *svāhā!*[15]

Not long after I received *śaktipāt*, I had an experience in meditation in which I was driving up Highway 101 in California between San Jose and San Francisco. The freeway signs were familiar: Palo Alto, Menlo Park, Burlingame. Then suddenly another sign loomed ahead — Death. And I calmly recognized that that was the exit I had to take — the death of the limited ego. I turned off on the cloverleaf and soon found myself on a dirt road in the country. Ahead of me was a blazing fire that extended clear across the road from one side to the other. I would have to go through it; there was no way around it. As I drove into the fire and was enveloped by flames, I came out of meditation. For years after that, whenever I was going through a particularly intense phase of purification, I would have a vision of being surrounded by those flames, and I knew it was the fire of the awakened Kundalini at work, burning up my impurities.

After taking an Intensive, also, I would invariably wake up the next morning to see my bed surrounded by flames. This vision was never frightening; I always understood what it meant and knew it was a great blessing.

On the physical level, the element of fire at the *maṇipūra chakra* is associated with the digestive fire. Lord Krishna tells Arjuna: "Having become the *vaiśvānara* fire, I abide in the body of all living beings and, associated with the *prāṇa* and *apāna*, digest the four kinds of food."[16]

Jnaneshwar Maharaj comments on this verse, saying:

> I have lit a fire around the navel of each living being, and I am that fire in the belly.
>
> Fanning this fire with the bellows of the incoming and outgoing breaths, great quantities of food can be consumed in the belly day and night.
>
> Whether food is dry or juicy, well cooked or burned, I digest the four kinds of food.
>
> In this way I am all creatures, the life which supports them, and the inner fire which is the chief means of life.[17]

Anāhata Chakra

The heart *chakra* is of the color of the red *bandhuka* flower and has twelve petals. The vermilion-colored letters on its petals are *kaṁ, khaṁ, gaṁ, ghaṁ, ṅaṁ, chaṁ, chhaṁ, jaṁ, jhaṁ, ñaṁ, ṭaṁ,* and *ṭhaṁ.* This is where the sages hear the mystical *anāhata-śabda,* the unstruck sound, from which the *chakra* derives its name. It emanates without any contact between two objects. It is the *śabda brahman,* the Absolute in the form of sound.

We have already mentioned the ten grades of *nāda*, the divine sounds one begins to hear when the heart center opens. Baba said, "At the stage when he hears the *nāda*, the yogi discovers an ability to dance. I would sometimes go at night to the top of a hill and dance for hours on end. What a wonderful divine feeling it was!"[18]

It is said that the *anāhata chakra* is like the celestial wish-fulfilling tree, granting whatever the supplicant asks; but it bestows even more, since it leads him to liberation.[19] This *chakra* is also the dwelling place of the individual soul in the form of a flame. The soul resembles the steady, tapering flame of a lamp in a place where there is no wind because it is unaffected by worldly activity, just as the flame is undisturbed by the wind.

Baba Muktananda often described the flame of the soul. He said: "Within the heart is a space the size of a thumb, and here a divine light shimmers. The sages have spent their lives looking at this light. How marvelous is the heart center! How magnificent is the light in the heart space! How divine is the Goddess Kundalini! As She unfolds, man's entire being is transformed."[20]

The individual soul is called *haṁsaḥ*, a word rich in meaning. These two syllables represent Shiva and Shakti. *Haṁ* is Shiva, the *puruṣa* or experiencing subject, the *bindu,* the point into which everything is absorbed, the inbreath. *Sah* is Shakti, *prakriti* or primordial nature, *visarga* (emanation or creation), the outgoing breath. *Haṁsah* is the union of these two opposites, of male and female. *Haṁsah* also means "swan" in Sanskrit, hence the frequent representation of the soul as a swan.

Shankaracharya says: "I worship in the *anāhata chakra* that unique pair of swans who are *Haṁ* and *Sah*, swimming in the minds of great beings, who subsist entirely on the honey of the full-blown lotus of knowledge. By meditating on them, the seeker acquires knowledge of all the eighteen sciences and is able to extract the good from the bad, just as the swan separates milk from water."[21]

The swan is said to have the ability to separate milk from water, so it is a symbol of discrimination. In the same way, a wise person can discern good from evil, right from wrong, the permanent from the impermanent.

The *anāhata chakra* is the center of the air *tattva*, represented by the hexagonal *maṇḍala* composed of two interlacing triangles. The *maṇḍala* is the color of smoke, which emanates from the flame of the soul. The seed letter of air is *yaṁ,* and it is seated on a black antelope, which is noted for its fleetness. It is the vehicle of Vayu, the Vedic lord of the wind, with its property of motion. Because the element of air has this characteristic of movement, it stimulates the sense of touch, so the power of feeling by touch (*sparśendriya*) and touch-as-such (*sparśa tanmātra*) are connected with this center, together with the power of reproduction and sexual enjoyment (*upaṣthendriya*).

Located within the seed letter is Isha, the deity who oversees the first three *chakras*. Since he is a form of Shiva, he is depicted with three eyes, the third being the Eye of Wisdom, the fully opened *ājñā chakra* at the space between the eyebrows. He is described as "the beautiful One possessed of the soft radiance of ten million moons, and shining with the radiance of his matted hair." The Shakti of this center is Kakini, associated with the bodily substance of fat.

The golden *bāṇa liṅgam*, representing Shiva, is placed within an inverted triangle, denoting Shakti, "whose tender body is like ten million flashes of lightning." This is the site of the *Viṣṇu granthi*, the second of the three knots, the knot of the heart. This is also the region of the sun, whose rays tinge the filaments surrounding the lotus.

The *Śiva Saṁhitā* says: "In the *anāhata chakra* there is the *bāṇa liṅgam* and a beautiful flame. By contemplating it, a yogi attains wealth from both the visible and invisible realms."[22]

Whereas the qualities of the lower *chakras* are all negative, those of the *anāhata chakra* are mixed. Along with anxiety, the sense of mineness, arrogance, languor, conceit, covetousness, duplicity, indecision, and regret, we also find hope, endeavor, and discrimination.

Below the pericarp of this *chakra* is a small red, eight-petaled lotus known as *ānanda-kaṇḍa*. This is where mental worship on one's chosen deity should be performed. It is visualized as containing the wish-fulfilling tree with a jeweled altar beneath it, and the seat of the patron deity under a beautiful awning, surrounded by trees laden with flowers and fruit and sweet-voiced birds.

One woman had a vision of her heart as a desert, a dry and barren land. When she received *śaktipāt*, however, she was filled with love and began to weep. She saw her tears falling like rain on the desert, and they made it green and fertile. Sometimes our lives may feel like a desert, arid and meaningless. But the Shakti is the energy of enthusiasm, of greatness, of joy, and She stirs the heart of every creature. When She awakens within us, our lives take on profound significance.

The opening of the heart can come when one least expects it. I went to Gurudev Siddha Peeth to meet Baba Muktananda in 1973. It was July and the middle of the monsoon. On the third day after my arrival, I was assigned the *seva* (selfless service to the Ashram) of sweeping up the leaves in the lower garden, which actually amounted to picking them up by hand, one by one, out of the mud. At one point that afternoon, I glanced up and noticed that Baba and a small group of men were walking down the path toward me. Baba was making his daily rounds of the garden.

I stopped for a few minutes to watch him striding briskly along. Suddenly, he reached up and picked a leaf off one of the eucalyptus trees that lined the garden path in those days. He put the leaf in his mouth and began to chew it. Then he took it out of his mouth, blew on it, and began to chew it again. "How peculiar," I thought. He kept doing this — chewing on the leaf, then taking it out of his mouth and blowing on it. Abruptly, he turned off the path, walked over to me, took the leaf out of his mouth, and handed it to me without saying a word. Then he walked on. I was dumbstruck! I managed to stammer, "Thank you, Baba!" I was flattered at his attention, but I had no idea what the gesture had meant, or why he had done such a strange thing.

Later on, I came to understand that Baba had infused that leaf with his Shakti, his spiritual power, and to this day I've kept the leaf preserved among my most precious treasures.

It was time for a chant in the temple, and I went in a few minutes early just to sit quietly. I was still holding the leaf. Almost immediately, there was a tremendous crash right above the top of my head. It sounded like an airplane breaking through the sonic barrier. Simultaneously, an explosion took place in my chest, as if dynamite had blasted open a granite boulder. Intense waves of love began to course through me, and I burst into tears.

I cried for two weeks — which was about the length of time it took me to adjust to my new condition, for it didn't go away; those waves of love kept washing over me, within me, through me. They made all the love I had felt before that time seem like a pale, weak relative of what I was now experiencing. This new love was far more intense, totally pure, and unconditional.

I remembered the Spanish mystics whose works I had read in graduate school. At the time I had been unable to relate to them at all. But now they flashed vividly before my mind. "This is what they were talking about," I thought. "This is divine love. My God — it's real!"

Those intense waves of love kept surging through me, twenty-four hours a day, uninterruptedly, for about a year and a half; then they became sporadic. During that time, I slept very little. I didn't want to sleep, to become unconscious, unaware of that love. I would lie awake in the dorm, staring into the velvety blackness of the tropical night, savoring that indescribable experience that had been so freely given to me.

Baba once said, "As you meditate more and more, your heart will begin to overflow with love. You will get into a state in which you laugh like one who is mad. I am not telling you to become mad; I am only telling you that love and happiness should come forth spontaneously from inside you. God is joy."[23]

The great Sufi poet-saint, Jalaluddin Rumi, wrote so beautifully and with such intensity of the experience of divine love. He said that ecstatic love is an ocean, and that the Milky Way is just a flake of foam floating on it.

Viśuddha Chakra

This is the fifth *chakra* and it is located in the throat. The scriptures say that because the individual soul attains purity by seeing the Self in the heart, this *chakra* is called *viśuddha* (pure). It is of a smoky purple hue, and its sixteen petals bear the crimson-colored vowels: *aṁ, āṁ, iṁ, īṁ, uṁ, ūṁ, riṁ, rīṁ, lriṁ, lrīṁ, eṁ, aiṁ, oṁ, auṁ, aṁ* (the inbreath — *bindu* and Shiva), and *aḥ* (the outbreath — *visarga* and Shakti). The vowels are visible to one whose intellect has been purified through yogic practice. There are no psychological qualities associated with these petals. Instead, there are seven subtle tones, certain *bīja* mantras; in the eighth petal there is venom, and in the sixteenth there is nectar, which represent the destructive and upbuilding forces of the world.

This is the center of the ether *tattva*, which is represented by a white circle, the *maṇḍala* of the ether principle. The seed letter of ether is *haṁ*. It is white, clothed in space, and is represented as seated on its vehicle, a snow-white elephant. The element of ether or space stimulates the sense of hearing, so the power of hearing (*śravaṇendriya*) and sound-as-such (*śabda tanmātra*) are associated with the *viśuddha chakra*, together with the power of speaking (*vāgendriya*).

In the *bindu* of *haṃ* is Sadashiva, the deity of the *chakra*, in his androgynous form as half Shiva and half Shakti. He is described as "the great snowwhite deva, three-eyed and five-faced, with ten beautiful arms, and clothed in a tiger's skin. His body is united with that of Girija; and he is known by what his name, Sadashiva, signifies (the Beneficent One)."[24]

The left half of his body is of a golden color, and the right half is silver. He is to be visualized as sitting on a great lion seat that is placed on the back of a bull. The bull is the vehicle of Shiva, and the lion is the vehicle of Shakti.

The *devī* of the *chakra* is the white Shakti Sakini, whose form is light. Because bone is the bodily substance that she represents, she is pictured as seated on bones. She is found in the region of the moon in the center of the lotus. Whereas the *maṇipūra chakra* is the region of fire and *anāhata* is the region of the sun, *viśuddha* is the region of the moon. It is described as "the moon without the mark of the hare," the marks on the moon that children sometimes call "the man in the moon." In other words, the moon here is stainless and unblemished. This lunar region is referred to as "the gateway of the Great Liberation" for those who have purified and conquered their senses.

One who concentrates on this lotus becomes "a great sage, eloquent and wise, and enjoys uninterrupted peace of mind. He sees the three periods (past, present, and future) and becomes the benefactor of all, free from disease and sorrow, long-lived, and the destroyer of endless dangers."[25]

The *viśuddha chakra* is the dwelling place of Saraswati, the goddess of speech, and when Kundalini becomes active here She may awaken in a yogi divine vocal powers that have been previously dormant. The biblical story of Pentecost is an example of a *varṇamayī* manifestation operating at the *viśuddha chakra*. About forty days after Easter, all the apostles had gathered at one place. As they sat together, suddenly there came from heaven a noise like a rushing wind that filled the whole house. Then, in the midst of this sound and fury, tongues of flame appeared and settled on the head of each apostle. They were all filled with the Holy Spirit, and they began to speak in tongues with which they were unfamiliar. A huge crowd gathered, people from all over the world — Rome, Egypt, Libya, Greece, Crete — to hear what was going on. They were bewildered because the local people, who were Galileans, were speaking great spiritual truths in the native languages of the foreigners.

Gurumayi once said:

> *Viśuddha* is the region of *saṅdhi*, of transition. It is like twilight, where light and darkness exist together briefly, as one takes over from the other. It is the center where purity and impurity exist together. After seeing the soul in the center of *anāhata*, you have transcended the passions and negative emotions. The drama is behind you. And yet, you have not entirely transcended duality. From *viśuddha*, your awareness can either move down into the world of turbulent emotions, or it can rise higher into the realm of the magnificent virtues.[26]

Ājñā Chakra

In Baba Muktananda's words:

> As Kundalini keeps rising, as all the lower *chakras* are pierced, one's awareness comes to the space between the eyebrows, which is called the *ājñā chakra*. This *chakra* is also called the seat of the Guru. *Ājñā* means "command," and Kundalini will not move past this center without the command of the inner Guru...[27]
>
> There are very strict customs officials sitting at this point and regulating your entry into the higher realms. Ordinary customs officials are quite casual, because they let drugs pass through and various other things. But the customs authorities here are very stubborn, and they won't let any such thing pass.[28]

Baba continues:

> As the *ājñā chakra* is pierced, you experience the merging state of the mind. The mind becomes very still and one-pointed, and the thoughts that have created disturbances become quiet. This is the beginning of the final stage of *sādhana*, which leads to the ultimate attainment. After piercing through the *ājñā chakra*, Kundalini rises to the *sahasrāra*.[29]

The *ājñā chakra* is a lotus of two white petals, containing the white letters *haṁ* and *kṣaṁ*. *Haṁ* represents the final opening up of creation, and *kṣaṁ* is the letter that includes all of the other letters of the Sanskrit alphabet.[30] This implies that we have arrived at the end of the manifestation of the phenomenal universe. The seed letter of this *chakra* is *Oṁ*. We have now gone beyond the five material elements: earth, water, fire, air, and ether. This center is the seat of the subtle *tattvas* of mind and *prakriti*, primordial nature. *Prakriti* is the basic stuff of which the material universe is composed, a condensation of *māyā* that manifests the phenomenal world. And mind in this case includes the fourfold psychic instrument: the mind, subconscious mind, intellect, and ego.

The *Ṣaṭ Chakra Nirūpaṇa* states that this *chakra* "shines with the glory of meditation."[31] As the Shakti works in this center the mind becomes quiet, stable, and pure. Meditation now comes spontaneously. This is why the scriptures on *haṭha yoga* say that *rāja yoga*, the royal path, begins here.

Gurumayi said:

> When you go deep into meditation or when you start meditating with the awakened Shakti, you feel incredible pressure in your forehead. Sometimes it feels as if it is going to burst open. Many times, you can feel heat coming out of the forehead. If you are

> a deep meditator, then the energy is very concentrated in the space between the eyebrows. You can hardly open your eyes. It is as though something is resting on your eyelids and you have no power to open them at all. Sometimes it is so cool, very, very soothing. Whenever it is very concentrated in this space between the eyebrows, there is a buzzing sound. It is as if somebody were drilling a hole there or millions of bees were swarming in the space. At times, it gets very intense. However, you should not be afraid. With the awakened Shakti, this happens spontaneously.[32]

The two petals and the pericarp of the lotus represent the three *guṇas*: *sattva*, purity and light; *rajas*, passion and activity; and *tamas*, darkness and inertia. The deity of this *chakra* is Shambhu, another form of Shiva, and the Shakti is Hakini, representing the substance of marrow. There is the lightning-like *itara liṅgam,* set in an inverted triangle denoting Shakti. *Itara* means "that which enables one to cross the world of wandering." This is the site of the Rudra *granthi,* the final knot that must be opened before the seeker can enter the higher realms.

The *ājñā chakra* is also referred to as *mukta-triveṇi,* for it is here that the *īḍā* (Ganga), *piṅgalā* (Yamuna), and *suṣumnā* (Saraswati) once again converge. The term in Sanskrit means "the confluence of freedom."

The sacred syllable *Oṁ* is situated in a second triangle above the one in which the *itara liṅgam* rests. It is the inner Self in the form of the purified intellect and resembles a wickless flame because of its radiance. This is a beautiful vision that one can see in meditation.

The *Ṣaṭ Chakra Nirūpaṇa* states: "When the yogi closes the house which hangs without support, the knowledge of which he has gained by the service of his excellent Guru, and when the mind by repeated practice becomes dissolved in this place which is the abode of uninterrupted bliss, he then sees in the middle of and in the space above the triangle sparks of fire shining distinctly."[33]

This means that when the mind's connection with the world has been removed and when, as a result of meditation on *Oṁ*, the mind dissolves or merges here at the *ājñā chakra*, he sees sparks of light resembling fire within and above the triangle on which *Oṁ* rests. "The flame-like Self, auspicious and in the shape of *Oṁ*, is surrounded on all sides by sparks of light."[34]

The next verse continues: "He then also sees the light which is in the form of a flaming lamp. It is lustrous like the clearly shining morning sun and glows between the sky and the earth. It is here that supreme Shiva manifests Himself in the fullness of His might. He knows no decay and witnesses all, and is here as He is in the region of fire, moon, and sun."

In his commentary on this verse, Kalicharana explains that the phrase "glows between the sky and the earth" means that by its own luster it makes visible everything between the *mūlādhāra* and the *sahasrāra*. Paramashiva can be seen here in the *ājñā chakra* as well as in the *sahasrāra*. Shiva and Shakti are in union here in the *parabindu*, the Blue Pearl, represented by the *bindu* or dot over the *Oṁ*. This is the double of the *parabindu* which is in the *sahasrāra*. The Blue Pearl can also be experienced at this center as it shoots in and out of the eyes with great speed. The region of fire, moon, and sun refers to the *a-ka-tha* triangle in the *sahasrāra*.

It is here in the *ājñā chakra* that the yogi "joyfully places his *prāṇa* at the time of death and enters that supreme, eternal, birthless, primeval Deva, the *puruṣa*, who was before the three worlds, and who is known by Vedanta."[35]

Kalicharana elaborates at considerable length on this process of placing the *prāṇa* at the time of death. In brief, Kundalini is led upward through the different *chakras* to the *ājñā chakra*. "There the yogi dissolves all the diverse elements from the gross to the subtle in Kundalini. Last of all, he unites Her and the individual soul with the *bindu*, whose substance is Shiva and Shakti; then he pierces the *brahmārandhra* (at the crown of the head), leaves the body, and becomes merged in the Absolute."

Notes to Chapter 7

1 *Songs of Kabir*, translated by Rabindranath Tagore (New York: Samuel Weiser, 1974) 8:1:101, p. 52.
2 See Swami Vishnu Tirtha Maharaj, *Devātma Shakti*, 5th edition, 1980 (Rishikesh: Muni Ki Rati, 1948), pp. 88-94.
3 Pandit Ananta Krishna Shastri, *Saundarya Laharī* (Madras: Ganesh and Company, 1957), p. 29.
4 The English translation has been taken from *The Serpent Power*, by Sir John Woodroffe (first published, 1919; 7th edition, Madras: Ganesh and Company), 1964.
5 Ibid. The commentary is included with the text itself.
6 See the *Adhyātmaviveka*, quoted in the *Dīpikā* to verse 7 of the *Haṁsah Upaniṣad*.
7 See Appendix.
8 *Ṣaṭ Chakra Nirūpaṇa* 10-11.
9 Unpublished talk, August 24, 1993.
10 See *The Serpent Power*, p. 13.
11 Unpublished talk, August 25, 1993.
12 *Ṣaṭ Chakra Nirūpaṇa* 18.
13 *Ṣaṭ Chakra Nirūpaṇa* 21.
14 Unpublished talk, August 25, 1993.
15 *Kaulāvalī Nirṇaya* 3:85.
16 *Bhagavad Gītā* 15:4.
17 *Jnaneshwar's Gītā* 15:375-378.
18 Swami Muktananda, *Play of Consciousness*, translated by Swami Chidvilasananda, 3d printing, 1987 (New York: SYDA Foundation, 1974), p. 163.

19 From a commentary on the *Ṣaṭ Chakra Nirūpaṇa* by Shankara, who lived at least eight centuries after the great Shankaracharya.
20 *Play of Consciousness*, p. 8.
21 *Ānanda Laharī* 38.
22 *Śiva Samhitā* 5:84
23 Swami Muktananda, *Where Are You Going?* (New York: SYDA Foundation, 1981), p. 101.
24 *Ṣaṭ Chakra Nirūpaṇa* 29.
25 Ibid., 31.
26 Unpublished talk, August 27, 1993.
27 Swami Muktananda, *Kundalini, The Secret of Life*, 2d edition (New York: SYDA Foundation, 1979), p. 37.
28 Swami Muktananda, *From the Finite to the Infinite* (New York: SYDA Foundation, 1986), vol 2, p. 86.
29 *Kundalini, The Secret of Life*, p. 32.
30 See Kshemaraja's commentary on the *Śiva Sūtras* 2:17.
31 *Ṣaṭ Chakra Nirūpaṇa* 32.
32 Swami Chidvilasananda, "Making the Moon and the Sun Rise," *Darshan* magazine 41/42 (1990), p. 85.
33 *Ṣaṭ Chakra Nirūpaṇa* 36.
34 See Kalicharana's commentary on verse 36.
35 Ibid., 38.

Great beings whose minds are free from māyā effortlessly see Thy abode wherein are the sun, moon, and fire, which is as subtle as a flash of lightning, and which is placed above the six lotuses in the forest of the great lotus. Seeing this, they are immersed in a wave of supreme bliss.

—*Ānanda Laharī* 21

CHAPTER 8

THE SAHASRARA:

Merging with the Immensity

The scriptures say that when the yogi's actions are good in all respects, through service to his Guru, then he rises above the *ājñā chakra*. The region between *ājñā* and the *sahasrāra* at the crown of the head is the seat of the causal body. Whereas the Shaktis below the *ājñā chakra* are looking forward towards creation, the Shaktis above *ājñā* are looking backward towards dissolution, and are liberating forces.

The yogi has been meditating intensely on the primordial Oṁ in the *ājñā chakra*, and as a result of this, there follow nine causal Shaktis that are stages or subtle levels of sound, or *nāda*. In ascending order they are *bindu (or ardha matra), ardha chandra, rodhini, nāda, nādānta, shakti, vyāpini, samāna,* and *ūnmanī*.[1] Each stage is subtler than the previous one. It is as though the sound of Oṁ leaves a trail behind it. It becomes subtler and finer, until finally it disappears altogether, taking one's consciousness with it to the *ūnmanī* state beyond the mind.

In Tibet, this is a common visualization and form of meditation — the flame at the *ājñā chakra*, becoming finer and finer as it rises, until it disappears into a wisp at the very tip, leading one beyond the mind to pure Consciousness.

Up to *samāna* there is *atmā-vyāpti,* realization of the

inner Self. It is only at the stage of *ūnmanī* that *Śiva-vyāpti* occurs — not only realization of the Self, but also the realization that the whole world is an aspect of the Self. Even in *samāna* there is still the play of *māyā*, with residual traces of thoughts and desires. Only at the *ūnmanī* stage does *māyā* cease completely and one enters Shiva Consciousness. This is the *sahaja* or natural state of *samādhi*.[2] Gurumayi said:

> This is the goal of meditation and contemplation. When all the impurities are washed away, you begin to perceive the luminous Self. As this awareness gradually becomes clearer and clearer, you can live a good and worthy life.
>
> When you receive blessings from a Guru, a state of awareness arises. It is the pure awareness, "I am. I am all there is, I am all that is and all that is not — I am." A Guru has seen the Truth. A Guru lives in the Truth. The Truth is "I am," "I am the Truth."
>
> The divine pulsation, "I am, I am." The scintillating Blue Pearl, "I am, I am." The culmination of all yoga, "I am, I am." All this is revealed within. And once that perfection permeates your being, you live in that experience all the time; there is no return.[3]

As we ascend into the *sahasrāra*, we enter a region that is inconceivable by the mind and indescribable in speech. Nevertheless, once we come down from it, we retain aspects of that experience which we can try to talk about. The Sanskrit word *sahasrāra* means "one thousand," for this supreme lotus has a thousand petals. The *sahasrāra* is the realm of pure Consciousness. It is lustrous and whiter than the full moon, and its filaments are tinged with the color of the rising sun. On its petals are all the fifty letters of the Sanskrit alphabet, white in color, and repeated twenty times. It is the source of absolute bliss.

We have already seen that the seat of the individual soul, *haṁsah*, is the *anahata* or heart *chakra*. The *sahasrāra* is the seat of the Supreme Self, *Parama Haṁsah*. It is here that we realize the oneness of the individual soul and the Supreme Soul. This Supreme *Haṁsah* is the all-powerful Great Light that devours the universe. It is also the Guru Principle.

The *Pādukā Pañchaka* says:

> I meditate on the Guru in the lotus of a thousand petals, which is radiant like the cool rays of the full moon, whose lotus hands make the gestures which grant blessing and dispel fear. His raiment, garland, and perfumes are ever fresh and pure. His countenance is benign. He is in the *Haṁsah* in the head. He is the *Haṁsah* Himself.[4]

The scriptures say that there is an upward-turned lotus of twelve petals, which is immediately below the pericarp of the downward-turned *sahasrāra* and inseparable from it. Where the two pericarps meet, there is the *maṇḍala* of the full moon, and within this is the *a-ka-tha* triangle mentioned in the *Guru Gītā*:

> In the round space of the thousand-petaled lotus, there is a triangular lotus which is formed by the three lines beginning with *a, ka,* and *tha,* and which has *haṁ* and *sah* on two sides. One should remember the Guru, who is seated in its center.[5]

A woman said that shortly after she received *śaktipāt*, her body would vibrate with energy and she would utter odd sounds: "*a-ka-tha...a-ka-tha...a-ka-tha...a-ka-tha... Haṁsah...Guru Oṁ.*" Then she would dissolve in bliss. This went on for a year, and she enjoyed it immensely, although she did not understand the significance of it. Then, while chanting this verse of the *Guru Gītā* one day, she glanced at the translation and saw it all spelled out for her. "What an incredible yoga," she thought, "that through the Guru's grace we can actually experience what the scriptures speak of."

The sixteen Sanskrit vowels beginning with *a* form the first line of this triangle, the first sixteen consonants beginning with *ka* form the second line, and the sixteen consonants beginning with *tha* form the third. The remaining letters *ha, lla,* and *kṣa* are located in the angles. The first is the line of fire, and since fire is considered the origin of life, this line is associated with Brahma, creation, and *rajo guṇa*. The second is the line of the moon, connected with Vishnu, preservation, and *sattva guṇa*. The third is the line of the sun, representing the twelve suns that rise to burn the world at the time of dissolution, so it is associated with Rudra, destruction, and *tamo guṇa*. The one Shakti becomes three in order to perform these various functions. In the scriptures, the *sahasrāra* is often called the region of sun, moon, and fire, and it is this triangle that they are referring to.

The *a-ka-tha* triangle is the abode of Shakti and also of Paramashiva, the supreme Guru. The place of the Guru is on a jeweled altar within this triangle, and when a seeker meditates on the Guru's feet, it is here that they are found. The *Pādukā Pañchaka* says:

> I adore in my head the two lotus feet of the Guru. The jeweled footstool on which they rest removes all sin. They are red like young mango leaves. Their nails resemble the moon shining in all her glory. Theirs is the beautiful luster of lotuses growing in a lake of nectar.[6]

The Guru's feet are cool like the nectarean beams of the moon, for just as moonbeams counteract heat, devotion to the Guru's feet overcomes sorrow and suffering.

In the very center of this triangle is the Blue Pearl, or *parabindu*. This scintillating blue dot is sometimes called the "cosmic creative drop," for it is the state of the gathered-up power of Consciousness that is about to create the universe. The Blue Pearl "sprouts" into three pearls, or *bindus*, and the lines connecting them form the *a-ka-tha* triangle. This triangle, composed of all the letters of the alphabet, is the source of all sound vibration; then these sounds or letters come down in sequence through the *chakras*. The entire universe of vibrating sound is evolved from the Blue Pearl.

Gurumayi said:

> Meditate on the Guru in the form of the Blue Pearl. It sits in the center of a vibrating triangle in the thousand-petaled lotus of the *sahasrāra*. You do not necessarily see only one Blue Pearl at a time; sometimes you see thousands and thousands of blue dots. The vision of the Blue Pearl is very intoxicating. In fact, it has the ability to remove the deepest sorrows in your heart. When suffering starts leaving you, you are able to hear the sound *Oṁ* and you become new. All that is old in your being goes away; you become very lighthearted. You can almost feel what God feels.[7]

The scriptures say that the Blue Pearl is very secret and subtle, like the end of a hair that has been divided ten million times. It is the source of a mass of great bliss, which is liberation. In the center of the Blue Pearl is the Great Void, the *mahā śūnya*, where the union of Shiva and Shakti finally takes place.

The *Tantrāntara* says: "The king among yogis becomes full of the bliss of the Absolute by making his mind the abode of the Great Void, which is set in the light of the sun, moon, and fire."[8]

The Great Void should not be confused with the void that is associated with the state of deep sleep and the causal body, in which lie all the seeds of ignorance and of our future *karmas*. The *mahā śūnya* is the Absolute, the Supreme, the Immensity. It is not merely an empty space where objects are absent; it is actually full, for it is the source of all manifestation.

Baba says:

> The Blue Pearl is subtler than the subtlest. It is the size of a sesame seed. Yet even though it is so tiny, it is very big; for this whole world of movable and immovable things is contained within it... Within the Blue Pearl are millions and millions of universes...
>
> Having perceived this truth directly, Tukaram Maharaj, a great saint of India, wrote, "The Lord of the universe builds a tiny house the size of a sesame seed and lives inside it. All the different gods — Brahma, Vishnu, and Mahesh — come and go inside this tiny house." [9]

Within the *maṇḍala* of the moon in the *sahasrāra* can be found the mysterious "pot of nectar," which the poet-saints and mystics speak of. Kalicharana explains that the moon has fifteen phases that are known and two that are secret. These last two phases, the sixteenth and seventeenth, are called *amā-kalā* and *nirvāṇa-kalā*, respectively.[10] They are very subtle and can only be revealed in meditation. They have the shape of a delicate crescent moon and are downward-turned. They are the source of the stream of nectar flowing from the *sahasrāra* down through the *suṣumnā*. This divine nectar has its origin in the blissful union of Shiva and Shakti. Baba describes it very beautifully:

> Just as the rain follows thunder in the atmosphere, the same thing happens in the inner spaces. When

> the thunder (the *megha nāda*) sounds in the inner spaces,… a shower of nectar begins to fall. There is a pool of nectar behind the forehead, and… this nectar is released and drops onto the root of the tongue. When the inner nectar touches the tongue, the taste buds become extremely refined; then, even if you eat the simplest food, you relish it as pure elixir. When the inner nectar travels down to the gastric fire in the solar plexus, it spreads through all the nerves. This nectar nourishes the body so that it is not necessary to consume much food.[11]

When this nectar is released, it flows through all the *nāḍīs* and rejuvenates the body. Jnaneshwar Maharaj describes how the body is transformed once this nectar begins to flow. He says:

> When heated metal is poured into a mold,
> the wax of the mold melts and pours out;
>
> And only the metal remains,
> taking the form of the mold.
>
> Similarly, beauty incarnates in the form of the body,
> covered by a veil of skin.
>
> The beauty of the limbs looks like natural marble or
> the sprouting of seed jewels,
>
> As if the lovely hues of the evening
> sky were transferred to the body,
>
> Or as if an image were fashioned
> from the inner radiance of the spirit.
>
> This is how the yogi's body appears
> when Kundalini has drunk of the nectar.
>
> The god of death is even afraid to look at it.
>
> Old age vanishes, the knot of youth is loosened, and

> the lost bloom of childhood reappears.
>
> Like ever-new jewel buds opening on the boughs
> of a tree of gold, fine new fingernails grow.
>
> Over the whole body, tiny new hairs
> spring forth like small splinters of rubies.
>
> The palms of the hands and the soles of the feet are
> like red lotus flowers, and the eyes shine with an
> indescribable luster.[12]

Some years ago an Australian housewife went up in the *darśan* line during an evening program at the South Fallsburg Ashram. After she had pranamed to Baba, she returned to her place and became locked in meditation. There was some force, she said, that was trying to escape, like a root cracking through concrete. It was in the form of a cobra. It rose up to the heart area, where there was an exquisite lotus that was fully open. Her entire being turned blue. Then she became aware of something white on the crown of her head. She saw it was a white lotus, enormous like a cathedral, which had hundreds of petals, all vibrating and creating a chorus-like sound. At the tip of each petal was a golden jewel drop. Something was dripping from the crown of her head down through her body; it was like honey, but not sticky. Her whole being said, "This is grace." She was new to Siddha Yoga and was completely unaware of the significance of this experience.

The *Śiva Saṁhitā* says:

> By seeing the region of the moon in the *sahasrāra*, all the planets become auspicious, all dangers are destroyed, all accidents are avoided, success in one's endeavors is attained, and all powers are acquired. By the constant practice of yoga, one attains perfection and becomes equal to Shiva.[13]

Thc *Ṣaṭ Chakra Nirūpaṇa* describes very poetically the rising of Kundalini into the *sahasrāra*:

> The *Devī*... having reached all the lotuses in the *suṣumnā nāḍī*, shines therein in the fullness of Her luster. Then, in Her subtle state, fine like the lotus fiber and lustrous like lightning, She goes to the gleaming flamelike Shiva, the Supreme Bliss, and suddenly produces the bliss of liberation.[14]

As Kundalini rises, She absorbs all the *tattvas* of creation into Herself as if She were rolling up a mat. This is the process of *laya*, absorption or merging. The element of earth with the sense of smell and its associated *tattvas* in the *mūlādhāra chakra* dissolve into water at *svādhiṣṭhāna*, the element of water and the sense of taste are absorbed into fire at *maṇipūra*, fire and the sense of sight merge into air at *anāhata*, air and the sense of touch merge into ether at *viśuddha*, ether and the sense of hearing are absorbed into the mind and the other psychic instruments at *ājñā*, and finally the mind dissolves into the Self at the *sahasrāra*.

Shri Shankaracharya describes it like this:

> My mind fell like a hailstone into that vast expanse of the ocean of the Supreme. Touching one drop of it, I melted away and became one with the Absolute. And now I abide in the joy of the Self.[15]

An interesting point the scriptures make is that Kundalini rises to the *sahasrāra* and returns to the *mūlādhāra* at the base of the spine, again and again, until She ultimately becomes stabilized in the *sahasrāra* and does not return. This accounts for the brilliant halos that artists depict around the heads of the saints. After Kundalini has stabilized in the *sahasrāra*, as in the case of a Siddha, She can still play within the pure area of unity-awareness between the *sahasrāra* and the *ājñā chakra*, but She no longer comes down through *māyā* below the *ājñā chakra*. While we are still doing *sādhana*, we can have occasional experiences of the *sahasrāra*, but we again plunge back down through *māyā*. As Kundalini returns to Her place in the *mūlādhāra chakra* along the pathway of the *suṣumnā*, She again rolls out the mat of creation and all the *tattvas* and elements associated with the *chakras* reappear as She descends through them. Her ascent was *laya-krama*, absorption or dissolution, and Her descent is *sriṣṭi-krama*, or creation:

> O Mother! After Your body has been moistened with the nectar flowing from the *sahasrāra*, You again reach Your dwelling in the *mūlādhāra* through the *suṣumnā*. O Mother and Spouse of Shiva! They in whose heart You glitter are never reborn.[16]

A few years ago I was in an Intensive. During the final session of meditation, I looked up and saw that the ceiling of the meditation hall had dissolved into brilliant white light. That light began to descend until it absorbed me into it. Suddenly, I had the sensation of breaking through a barrier. As I came out on the other side, I was in an entirely different state. I was all-pervasive and utterly free. There was nothing I could not do. And the ecstasy was indescribable.

After a short time, my ordinary mind tried to reassert itself. It began to play one of its old familiar tapes, then another and another. I could clearly see that with each tape, I was tying myself up, as if with a rope. Soon I was bound hand and foot, and I was back in my normal waking state. Now, I had always thought that my ordinary state was fine — I was happy enough and had a good life. But compared with this other, tremendously expanded state, it seemed very contracted and limited indeed. And I saw that it was my own mental conditioning that had bound me and brought me down; no one else had robbed me of my freedom.

The awakened Kundalini Shakti begins to weaken our old conditioning and to change the way we see ourselves. She shows us that we are not small; we are potentially infinite.

Some people have an experience of the final state when they receive *śaktipāt* and mistakenly think they are fully realized. This happened to one woman following an Intensive with Baba. It took her completely by surprise. "I wonder what I should do now?" she mused. "I really didn't expect this to happen so soon! Where do I go from here?" After some reflection, she decided to spend the rest of her life on one of her favorite beaches in Hawaii. Shortly thereafter, however, she found herself back in her old familiar state. She was crushed. What had she done wrong? How had such a fall occurred? She hadn't done anything wrong. She had been given a great gift — an unmistakable experience of the ultimate state. Now, the work of purification had to begin in earnest so that one day she could hold on to that state and not let it slip through her fingers.*

* A few years ago, I came across a very interesting article by an eminent psychiatrist. He said that our civilization has reached the stage where we can experience the first four *chakras*. He said, however, "We have not reached *viśuddha*....Therefore, it is rather bold to speak of the sixth *chakra*, which is of course completely beyond our reach, because we have not even arrived at *viśuddha*....To speak about the lotus of the thousand petals, the *sahasrāra* center, is quite superfluous because that is merely a philosophical concept with no substance whatever for us; it is beyond any possible experience."[17] I found this very interesting. There are many people who have experiences of the *sahasrāra* after receiving *śaktipāt*. It doesn't mean that they are established there, but they certainly reach that realm now and then. So we must understand and appreciate the grace that is available to us. To know a *śaktipāt* Guru and receive divine grace — there is nothing rarer on the face of this earth — or more precious.

A few years ago, a group of us went on a *yatra,* or pilgrimage, to Hardwar, a lovely town in northern India where the Ganges flows out onto the plains after descending from the Himalayas. Hardwar, like its neighbor Rishikesh, is a town of *sannyāsis,* orange-clad monks, whom you see everywhere you look, and the streets are lined with ashrams. One of the ashrams we visited was large and well-maintained, and the swami who was its director greeted us warmly. Many older men, all renunciants, lived there and spent their time engaged in scriptural study and discussion.

At one point the swami said to us, "Tell us about *śaktipāt.* I know that Baba and Gurumayi are *śaktipāt* Gurus, and we have read about it in the scriptures. But what is it like? What is your experience of it?"

So we began to share some of our experiences. Many of us were Westerners, and there was nothing extraordinary about our backgrounds. But we all had had profound experiences of the Self as a result of receiving the Guru's grace and the awakening of Kundalini. As we shared our stories, I could not help watching the faces of those elderly men, filled with longing and wistfulness. I can still see them in my mind's eye. In spite of all their spiritual practices and their years of austerities, their scriptural knowledge remained merely on the intellectual level; they had not had the direct, first-hand experiences we were describing. It was one of those moments when we realized how truly fortunate we were.

Whenever I contemplate these experiences, I remember Baba's words:

> O supremely beautiful and effulgent Kundalini! Through Your grace, even an ordinary person becomes blessed, and is able to see the Supreme Principle within himself.[18]

Describing the final attainment, Baba said:

> Just as a river, after flowing for a long time, merges in the ocean and becomes the ocean, when Kundalini has finished Her work and stabilized in the *sahasrāra*, you become completely immersed in God. All your impurities... are destroyed, and you take complete rest in the Self. The veil which made you see duality drops away, and you experience the world as a blissful play of Kundalini, a sport of God's energy. You see the universe as supremely blissful light, undifferentiated from yourself, and you remain unshakeable in this awareness. This is the state of liberation, the state of perfection.[19]

Baba explained that at first the Blue Pearl appears briefly, like a flash of lightning. It may shoot in and out of the eyes in an instant. Gradually, its brilliance increases and it stabilizes before your vision. Ultimately, you must penetrate the Blue Pearl. Gurumayi says:

> As you meditate and meditate, you feel hollow. You go deeper and deeper within yourself. As you go deeper... there comes a point, a tiny point; and through that, all of a sudden you understand everything. You are able to see everything. You are able to hear everything. You are able to go everywhere. It is an amazing state.[20]

One day the Blue Pearl explodes, and its light fills the universe, and you experience your all-pervasiveness. You lose the awareness of your own body, and merge with the body of God. The Shaivite scriptures speak of this, saying:

> The yogi is struck with awe, and in this astonishment he achieves the great expansion of Consciousness. Thus he, the best of yogis, becomes

> established at the highest level of Consciousness. He grasps it firmly and never loses it. Thus he is no longer subject to worldly existence, the continuing round of birth and death which inspires fear in all living beings, because its cause, his own impurity, no longer exists.[21]

In this tremendously expanded state, the yogi sees the world as his own body.[22] He sees no separation between himself and others. In fact, there are no "others;" there is only one Self.

A great being once described what it is like to live in this state: "I am so closely linked to you all that you are like parts of my body... I am always with each one of you, wherever you happen to be... Know for certain that whatever you think and do, whether you are near or far away, it never escapes my attention."[23]

This is the state that the *Śiva Sūtras* call *lokānandaḥ samādhi sukham* — "The bliss of the world is the ecstasy of samadhi."[24] Baba describes this state in a very sublime way, saying, "The yogi who looks upon the universe as his own body, drinks the nectar of ecstasy. He sees the vast variety of objects, shapes, and forms, the endless modifications around him, as diverse and yet one; for they all appear in his own Self trembling with its bliss."[25]

Baba used to say that wherever he looked he would see the soft, gleaming, blue rays of Consciousness pulsating in all his states, whether he was meditating, sleeping, eating, or bathing. If he focused his attention, forms and shapes would emerge from that scintillating light; then, when he relaxed his focus, the names and forms would again dissolve into the shimmering blue rays of Consciousness.

The great poet-saint Tukaram Maharaj said, "I am drowning in inner bliss, and I see it reflected all around me. When this bliss arises within, one enters an entirely different realm where supreme bliss pervades everywhere. It stretches above and below, from east to west, from north to south. It is lapping on all sides. What should or shouldn't I do now? My refuge is now the feet of my Guru."

Gurumayi continually reminds us that this path is not just about feeling good, or attaining some lesser goals. This path is for *mokṣa*, liberation — the highest aim of human existence. And she tells us that this state is attainable. Once we receive *śaktipāt*, we have the Master to guide us. Now, we must have the commitment and the determination to travel the path to the end, and we must cooperate with the Guru in the task of patiently trimming away our small ego and limited notions of who and what we are. Although this may be uncomfortable or even painful at times, it is essential.

Shaivism says: "It is only a few who, blessed with the wealth of contemplation on the Absolute, ascend into the light of Shiva, which is their own true nature... Others, afflicted by egoism, do not do so."[26]

The *Ṣaṭ Chakra Nirūpaṇa* says:

> That most excellent of men who has controlled his mind and known the *sahasrāra* is never again born in the Wandering, the world of birth and death, as there is nothing in the three worlds that binds him to it. His mind being controlled and his aim achieved, he possesses complete power to do all that he wishes, and to prevent that which is contrary to his will. He is able to roam the inner spaces. His speech, whether in prose or verse, is ever pure and sweet.[27]

He is *jīvanmukta*, liberated though still living in a body, and attains *mokṣa* or *videha kaivalya*, bodiless liberation, when he leaves his physical body.

"The wheel is broken; the Desireless is attained. The river bed is dry; no water flows. No more will the broken wheel roll. This is the end of sorrow."[28]

This is the supreme state that awaits us at the culmination of the inner journey of Kundalini. May the Divine Mother ever bestow Her grace upon us.

Notes to Chapter 8

1 See introduction by Jaideva Singh to *Śiva Sūtras* translated and edited by Jaideva Singh (New Delhi: Motilal Banarsidas, 1979), p. xli.

2 See Kshemaraja's commentary on *Śiva Sūtras* 3:7.

3 Swami Chidvilasananda, "Creating a Body of Light," *Darshan* magazine, 41/42 (1990), p. 172.

4 Introductory verse to the *Pādukā Pañchaka* in *The Serpent Power*, by Sir John Woodroffe (first published, 1919; 7th edition, Madras: Ganesh and Company, 1964), p. 481.

5 *Guru Gītā* 58, in *The Nectar of Chanting* (New York: SYDA Foundation, 1975).

6 *Pādukā Pañchaka*, verse 6.

7 "Creating a Body of Light," p. 169.

8 From the commentary on *Ṣaṭ Chakra Nirūpaṇa* 52; see Woodroffe, *The Serpent Power*, (first published, 1919; 7th edition, Madras: Ganesh and Company, 1964), p. 467.

9 Swami Muktananda, *Kundalini, The Secret of Life*, 2d edition (New York: SYDA Foundation, 1979), p. 42.

10 See *Ṣaṭ Chakra Nirūpaṇa* 46-47.

11 *Kundalini, The Secret of Life*, pp. 39-40.

12 *Jnaneshwar's Gita* 6:249-50, 253-54, 259-60, 262, 264-65.

13 *Śiva Saṁhita* 5:150.

14 *Ṣaṭ Chakra Nirūpaṇa* 51.

15 *Viveka Chūḍāmaṇi* 482.

16 A rendering of *Bhuvaneśvarī* 10, from the *Tantrasāra*.

17 C. G. Jung, *Psychological Commentary on Kundalini Yoga* (Zurich: Spring Publications, 1976), pp. 6, 16-17.

18 *Kundalini Stavaha* (New York: SYDA Foundation, 1979).

19 *Kundalini, The Secret of Life*, pp. 44-45.

20 From an unpublished talk, October 1, 1984.

21 *Spanda Nirṇaya*.

22 *Śiva Sutras* 1:14.

23 Shri Ananda Mayi Ma, *Matri Darshan* (Germany: Mangalam Verlag S. Schang, 1983).

24 *Śiva Sutras* 1:18.

25 Swami Muktananda, *Siddha Meditation: Commentary on the Śiva Sutras and Other Sacred Texts* (New York: SYDA Foundation, 1979), p. 45.

26 *Spanda Sandoha.*

27 *Ṣaṭ Chakra Nirūpaṇa* 45.

28 *Udana*, a Buddhist scripture.

BABA MUKTANANDA'S

Prayer to Kundalini

O Goddess Kundalini!
You are red like the morning sun.
When You bestow Your grace,
the inner awakening takes place,
and You continually shower
the nectar of supreme bliss.

O Goddess!
Bestow Your compassionate
glance upon me.
When Your glance of grace
falls upon a human being,
he becomes God.

You are my own radiant,
joyful, supremely divine,
and all-pervading Self.

O Mother Kundalini!
Only Your gracious glance
can establish me
in my own Self.
Through Your blissful glance,
all beings live joyfully.

O Mother Kundalini!
manifest within me.

NOTE ON SANSKRIT TERMS

All Sanskrit terms and quotations are given in the standard scholarly transliteration style that is internationally employed, slightly modified to enable the reader to distinguish the pronunciation easily. Thus, *c* is shown as *ch*, and the semi-vowel *ṛ* is written as *ri*. For a detailed pronunciation guide, see *The Nectar of Chanting*, published by the SYDA Foundation.

APPENDIX

The Tattvas or Principles of Creation According to Kashmir Shaivism

The Tattvas of the Universal Experience

1. *Śiva Tattva*
2. *Śakti Tattva*
3. *Sadaśiva* or *Sadakhya Tattva*
4. *Īśvara Tattva*
5. *Śuddha Vidyā* or *Sad Vidyā Tattva*

The Tattvas of the Limited Individual Experience

6. *Māyā* — illusion, the veiling or obscuring force

The Five Kañchukas, or Cloaks

7. *Kalā* — limitation of omnipotence
8. *Vidyā* — limitation of omniscience
9. *Rāga* — limitation of completeness
10. *Kāla* — limitation of eternal existence
11. *Niyati* — limitation of omnipresence

The Tattvas of the Limited Individual

12. *Puruṣa*
13. *Prakriti*

The Tattvas of Mental Operation

14. *Buddhi* — intellect
15. *Ahaṁkāra* — ego
16. *Manas* — mind

The Tattvas of Sensory Experience

The Five Senses of Perception

17. *Śravaṇendriya* — the power of hearing
18. *Sparśendriya* — the power of feeling by touch
19. *Chakṣurindriya* — the power of seeing
20. *Rasanendriya* — the power of tasting
21. *Ghrāṇendriya* — the power of smelling

The Five Powers of Action

22. *Vāgendriya* — the power of speaking
23. *Upaṣthendriya* — the power of procreation and sexual enjoyment
24. *Payvindriya* — the power of excretion
25. *Hastendriya* — the power of handling
26. *Pādendriya* — the power of locomotion

The Five Tanmātras or Subtle Elements of Perception

27. *Śabda Tanmātra* — sound
28. *Sparśa Tanmātra* — touch
29. *Rūpa Tanmātra* — color
30. *Rasa Tanmātra* — flavor
31. *Gandha Tanmātra* — odor

The Tattvas of Materiality

The Five Gross Elements

32. *Ākāśa* — ether
33. *Vayu* — air
34. *Tejas* or *Agni* — fire
35. *Apas* — water
36. *Prithivi* — earth

Paramashiva, the Ultimate Reality, transcends all of these thirty-six *tattvas*. He is the Pure Consciousness unaffected by time or space, limitation or change, while existing as the foundation or substratum of all. Along with His transcendental aspect, however, He also has an immanent aspect that descends through the various principles of creation.

The first five *tattvas* comprise the Pure Creation. The true nature of the Divine has not yet been veiled. Shiva and Shakti are the eternal and mutually inseparable realities. The notion of a universe begins to emerge in the *sadaśiva tattva*, but it is vague and indistinct, still in the depths of Consciousness. It becomes more clearly defined in the *īśvara tattva* and increasingly so in the *śuddha vidyā tattva*, but there is no separation between the 'I,' or experiencing subject, and the object of experience, the universe.

The sixth *tattva*, *māyā* or illusion, creates a sense of differentiation. It makes the one Universal Consciousness appear to be broken up into duality and multiplicity. The *kañchukas*, or cloaks, the *tattvas* from seven to eleven, limit and shrink the powers of the Supreme. The result of *māyā* and the *kañchukas* is the creation of *puruṣa* and *prakriti*. The subject and the object have now split apart. *Puruṣa* is the individual soul, the limited subject who undergoes experience. *Prakriti* is what is experienced, the objective manifestation, with the three *guṇas* or qualities of nature. The *tattvas* of mental operation are fourteen through sixteen: the intellect, which ascertains or discerns; the ego, which identifies one as a particular person; and the mind, which builds up perceptions and concepts. The *tattvas* of sensory experience, seventeen through thirty-one, include the *indriyas*, which are not sense organs but powers which operate through the sense organs, and the *tanmātras*, or subtle elements of perception. The *tanmātras* themselves are abstract qualities which become perceptible only later in material objects. The senses have no meaning without their objects.

The *tattvas* of materiality, the gross elements, represent the greatest degree of limitation and contraction. Although they are found throughout the body, they have centers of force in their corresponding *chakras*. The element of earth represents all matter in a solid state, such as bones and muscles. Water includes liquids, such as urine and saliva. Fire manifests as hunger and thirst, heat and light. Air manifests as the breath. Ether spreads outward in all directions, radiating lines of force symbolized as the "Hair of Shiva." It is the space in which all the other forces operate. With the appearance of these final *tattvas*, the descent of the Supreme into matter is now complete.

GLOSSARY

Abhinavagupta: (ca. 950-1015): Commentator and exponent of Kashmir Shaivism. Of the lineage of Vasugupta and Somananda, and author of *Tantrāloka*, *Tantrasāra*, and *Iśvara Pratyabhijñā Vimarśinī*.

Advaya Taraka Upaniṣad: One of the one hundred eight *Upaniṣads* in the collection of the *Muktika Upaniṣad*.

Ājñā chakra: The spiritual center located between the eyebrows. The awakened Kundalini passes through this *chakra* only by the command (*ājñā*) of the Guru.

A-ka-tha triangle: A vibrating triangle in the *sahasrāra* composed of all the letters of the alphabet; the source of all sound.

Amā-kalā: The secret sixteenth phase of the moon; together with *nirvāṇa-kalā*, it is the source of the stream of nectar flowing from the *sahasrāra*.

Anāhata chakra: The spiritual center located at the heart. The unstruck (*anāhata*) sound heard in meditation originates in this center.

Ānanda-kāṇḍa: A red lotus of eight petals below the *anāhata chakra*; it is here that mental worship of one's chosen deity is performed.

Ānanda Laharī: "Wave of Bliss," a beautiful hymn of praise to the *Devī*; from the *Saundarya Laharī* by Shankaracharya. It deals with Kundalini, the *chakras*, and yoga, and gives the essence of *Śrī Vidyā*.

Arjuna: The third of the five Pandava brothers and one of the heroes of the *Mahābhārata*. It was to Arjuna that Krishna imparted the knowledge of the *Bhagavad Gītā*.

Āsana: Various bodily postures practiced to strengthen the body and purify the *nāḍīs*.

Ashram: A spiritual institution or community where spiritual discipline is practiced; the abode of a saint or holy being.

Baba: A term of affection for a saint or holy man, meaning "father."

Bandha: Lock; an exercise of *haṭha yoga*. The three main locks are *jālandhara bandha*, in which the head is bent forward and the chin is pressed against the chest; *uḍḍiyāna bandha*, in which the stomach muscles are pulled inward toward the spine; and *mūla bandha*, in which the anus is pulled inward.

Bhagavad Gītā: One of the essential scriptures of Hinduism, a portion of the *Mahābhārata*, in which Krishna instructs Arjuna on the battlefield on the nature of God, the universe, and the Self, on the different forms of yoga, and on the way to attain God.

Bhagawan: the Lord; a term of address for God or saints denoting the glorious, divine, venerable, and holy.

Bhastrikā: A form of *prāṇāyāma* known as the "bellows breathing," in which the breath is drawn forcefully in and out.

Bhuvaneśvarī: "Lady of the Spheres," one of the names of the *Devī*.

Bīja mantra: Seed letter, a basic sound from the Sanskrit language, the repetition of which manifests the object or deity that it represents.

Bindu: Dot or point; the Blue Pearl, a compact mass of Shakti gathered into an undifferentiated point, ready to manifest as the universe.

Blue Pearl: See *bindu*.

Brahma: The creator; one of the Hindu trinity of Brahma, Vishnu, and Shiva.

Brahmā-dvara: The "door to the Absolute," the entrance to the *suṣumnā nāḍī* at the *mūlādhāra chakra*.

Brahmā nāḍī: The "channel of the Absolute," the space within the *chitriṇī nāḍī* through which Kundalini passes.

Brahmāṇḍa: The macrocosm, the universe.

Brahmāraṇdhra: A subtle center in the crown of the head, at the fontanelle.

Causal body: The body in which the deep-sleep state is experienced, represented by a black light the size of a fingertip; its seat is in the heart.

Chaitanya: The fundamental Consciousness which is absolutely free; a *chaitanya* mantra is conscious or alive with Shakti.

Chakra: One of the six major energy centers in the *suṣumnā nāḍī*.

Chandi: A form assumed by the *Devī* to destroy the demon Chanda.

Chitriṇī: A subtle, moonlike *nāḍī* within the *suṣumnā*.

Darśan: Seeing or being in the presence of a saint, a deity, or a sacred place.

Devatā: Deity.

Devī: Goddess.

Devī Aparad Kṣamāpana Stotra: "May the *Devī* Grant Me Pardon," a hymn to the Divine Mother composed by Shankaracharya.

Dhātus: The various bodily substances: skin, blood, flesh, fat, bone, and marrow.

Dīkṣā: Initiation, the spiritual awakening of the disciple by *śaktipāt* through a look, word, thought, or touch of the Guru.

Divya Dīkṣā day: The day of divine initiation, when one receives *śaktipāt*.

Durga: One of the names of the Divine Mother. In Her personal form, She is portrayed as an eight-armed goddess who rides a lion and carries weapons to combat the demonic forces and our evil tendencies.

Evolution: The process initiated with *śaktipāt*; the path of return to the source, carried out by the awakened Kundalini.

Granthi: A knot in the *suṣumnā* which must be pierced by the awakened Kundalini. The three knots are: *Brahmā granthi* in the *mūlādhāra chakra*, *Viṣṇu granthi* in the *anāhata chakra*, and *Rudra granthi* in the *ājñā chakra*.

Gross or physical body: The body in which we experience the waking state. It is associated with a red aura the size of the physical body, and its seat is in the eyes.

Guṇas: The three basic qualities of nature. They are *sattva*—purity, light, goodness; *rajas* — activity, passion; and *tamas* — darkness, inertia, ignorance.

Gurudev Siddha Peeth: (Siddha Peeth, lit. "abode of the Siddhas") The main ashram of Siddha Yoga, and the site of the *samādhi* shrine of Baba Muktananda. It was founded in 1956, when Bhagawan Nityananda instructed Swami Muktananda to live in a simple three-room compound near Ganeshpuri, India.

Guru Gītā: The "Song of the Guru," a garland of mantras in the form of a dialogue between Shiva and Parvati, which explains the identity of the Guru with the Absolute and describes the nature of the Guru, the Guru-disciple relationship, and meditation on the Guru.

Haṁsah Upaniṣad: A Yoga *Upaniṣad* of the *Śukla Yajur Veda*, dealing with the *Haṁsah* and the *Paramahaṁsah*.

Haṁsah: The individual soul in the heart.

I Am: *Purno'ham vimarśa*, the perfect non-relational 'I'-consciousness.

Īḍā: The moon *nāḍī*, on the left side of the *suṣumnā*.

Involution: The process through which the Supreme descends into matter, from the subtle *tattvas* to the gross.

Jaḍa: Lifeless, inert. A *jaḍa* mantra has not been infused with Shakti by a Master.

Japa: Repetition of a mantra.

Jīvanmukta: One who is liberated while still in the physical body.

Jnaneshwar Maharaj (1275-1296): Foremost among the saints of Maharashtra and a child yogi of extraordinary powers. His verse commentary on the *Bhagavad Gītā*, the *Jnaneshwari*, in the Marathi language, is one of the world's most important spiritual works. He also composed a short work, the *Amritānubhav*, and over one hundred *abhangas*, or devotional songs in Marathi, which describe various spiritual experiences following the awakening of Kundalini.

Kabir (1440-1518): A great poet-saint who lived his life as a weaver in Benares.

Kāla: One of the five *kañchukas*. It is the cloak that limits the supreme Self's condition of eternal existence. It brings into being the sequential existence of things and the temporal order — past, present, and future.

Kalā: One of the five *kañchukas*. It limits the universal condition of omnipotence.

Kalāvati: One of the categories of the manifestation of awakened Kundalini. It involves the purification of the thirty-six *tattvas*, or principles of creation, and pertains to *laya yoga*.

Kali: The form of the Divine Mother that embodies the power of dissolution and destruction.

Kalicharana: Commentator on the *Ṣaṭ Chakra Nirūpaṇa* and the *Pādukā Pañchaka*.

Kañchukas: The cloaks that the Supreme voluntarily throws over Himself which limit and contract His powers.

Kāṇḍa: The bulb-shaped origin of all the *nāḍīs*, located between the anus and the reproductive organ.

Karma: Physical, verbal, or mental action.

Kashmir Shaivism: A nondual philosophy that recognizes the entire universe as a manifestion of Shakti, the divine conscious energy. It explains how the formless, unmanifest Supreme Principle manifests as the universe.

Kaulāvalī Nirṇaya: A Tantric text dealing with rituals, mantras, and *mudrās*.

Khecharī mudrā: A technique in *haṭha yoga* in which the tongue curls back upward against the palate and into the nasal pharynx, opening the way to the *sahasrāra*.

Krishna: The eighth incarnation of Vishnu, whose life story is described in the *Śrīmad Bhagavatam* and the *Mahābhārata*, and whose spiritual teachings are contained in the *Bhagavad Gītā*.

Kriyās: Bodily movements caused by the awakened Kundalini in order to purify the body and nervous system.

Kriyāvati: One of the categories of the manifestation of awakened Kundalini. It pertains to *haṭha yoga* and is characterized by spontaneous physical *kriyās* — *āsanas*, *bandhas*, *prāṇāyāma*, and *mudrās*.

Kshemaraja: The brilliant disciple of Abhinavagupta, who wrote a commentary on the *Śiva Sūtras* and composed the *Pratyabhijñāhridayam* and other important works of Kashmir Shaivism.

Kumbhaka: Voluntary or involuntary retention of the breath.

Kundalini: The primordial Shakti or cosmic energy that lies dormant in a coiled form in the *mūlādhāra chakra*. When She is awakened, She begins to move upward through the *suṣumnā*, piercing the *chakras* and initiating various yogic processes which purify and rejuvenate the entire being. When She enters the *sahasrāra* at the crown of the head, the individual soul merges into the universal Self.

Lakshmi: The goddess of wealth and prosperity and the consort of Vishnu.

Lalitā Sahasranāma: "The Thousand Names of Lalita," in the form of a dialogue between the sage Agastya and the god Hayagriva; the text has evolved from the *Brahmāṇḍa Purāṇa*.

Laya-krama: The process of absorption or dissolution; the upward journey of Kundalini.

Liberation: Freedom from the cycle of birth and death; the state of realization of oneness with the supreme Consciousness.

Madhya: The intermediate degree of intensity of *śaktipāt*.

Mahānirvāṇa Tantra: "The Tantra of the Great Liberation," which discusses liberation, the worship of the Absolute, *dharma* or righteous behavior, mantras, and rituals.

Mahārthamañjarī: A Shaivite text of the 12th century, composed by Maheshvarananda.

Mahā śūnya: The Great Void. It is emptiness in the sense that it is without manifest creation. It is not a state of nonexistence because it has the nature of Being, Consciousness, and Bliss Absolute.

Mahesh: A name of Shiva.

Mahiśarmardinī Stotra: A hymn to Durga as the powerful conqueror of demons. Mahisharmardini was the slayer of the demon Mahisha, who took the form of a buffalo.

Manda: The mildest degree of *śaktipāt*.

Maṇḍala: The geometric form which corresponds to a particular *tattva*, or principle of creation.

Maṇipūra chakra: The spiritual center located in the navel region.

Māyā: Illusion, the force that shows the unreal as real, and presents what is temporary and short-lived as eternal and everlasting.

Mokṣa: Liberation, freedom from the cycle of birth and death; the state of realization of oneness with the Absolute.

Mount Kailas: A mountain peak in the Himalayas in present-day Tibet, revered as the abode of Shiva; a name for the *sahasrāra* at the crown of the head.

Mudrās: Various advanced *haṭha yoga* techniques practiced to hold the *prāṇa* within the body and to force Kundalini to enter the *suṣumnā*; symbolic gestures and movements of the hands which express inner feelings and states.

Mūlādhāra chakra: The spiritual center at the base of the spine where Kundalini lies dormant and in a coiled form like a serpent.

Nāda: Inner divine music or sound.

Nāḍī: A channel of the subtle body which carries the *prāṇa* or vital force.

Nirvāṇa-kalā: The secret seventeenth phase of the moon; together with *amā-kalā*, it is the source of the stream of nectar flowing from the *sahasrāra* through the *suṣumnā*.

Niyati: One of the five *kañchukas*. It limits the universal condition of all-pervasiveness and gives rise to the limitation of space and causation.

Nyāsa: A yogic technique by which the subtle body is infused with *prāṇa*. This is done by touching particular areas of the body while reciting certain seed mantras.

Oṁ: The primal sound, from which the entire universe emanates.

Oṁ Namaḥ Śivāya: The mantra of the Siddha lineage, meaning "Salutations to Shiva," the inner Self. *Namaḥ Śivāya* has five syllables and is called the *pañchākṣari mantra*.

Pādukā Pañchakā: "Five-fold Footstool of the Guru," a short text of seven verses on the twelve-petaled lotus, which is inseparable from the pericarp of the *sahasrāra*.

Parā: The subtlest level of speech; the vibration of the Divine Mind that brings about the manifestation of the universe.

Parama Haṁsah: The supreme Self in the *sahasrāra*.

Paramārthasāra: A summary text by Abhinavagupta of some of the essential teachings of Kashmir Shaivism.

Parātriṃśika Vivaraṇa: Perhaps the most complex work of Abhinavagupta, a commentary on a set of verses said to form the concluding portion of the *Rudra Yamala Tantra*.

Piṇḍāṇḍa: The human body, the microcosm.

Piṅgalā: The sun *nāḍī*, on the right side of *suṣumnā*.

Play of Consciousness: Swami Muktananda's spiritual autobiography, delineating the entire journey of Kundalini from Her awakening to Her final merging with Shiva.

Prakriti: Primordial nature; the basic stuff of which the material world is made.

Prāṇa: The vital force.

Prāṇava: The word which refers to the mystic syllable *Oṁ*.

Prāṇāyāma: The regulation and control of the breath.

Pratyabhijñā: The doctrine of recognition of Kashmir Shaivism. A digest of this philosophy, called the *Pratyabhijñāhridayam*, was prepared by Kshemaraja, the disciple of Abhinavagupta.

Puruṣa: The individual soul, the experiencing subject.

Radha: The childhood companion and consort of Krishna, celebrated as the embodiment of devotion.

Rāga: One of the five *kañchukas*. It limits the universal condition of completeness and is the cause of attraction to particular objects or people.

Rama: The seventh incarnation of Vishnu, whose life story is told in the *Rāmāyaṇa*; a name of the all-pervasive supreme Reality.

Ramana Maharshi (1879-1950): The great sage of Arunachala, a sacred hill in South India.

Ramananda (15th century): A North Indian saint who revitalized the path of devotion in the north. Kabir, the weaver, was his disciple.

Rig Veda: See *Vedas*.

Rudra: A name of Shiva.

Rumi, Jalaluddin (1207-73): The most eminent poet-saint of Persia. After meeting Shams-i-Tabriz, an ecstatic wandering saint, he was transformed from a scholar into an intoxicated singer of divine love.

Sādhana: The practice of spiritual discipline.

Sahaja samādhi: The natural state of *samādhi*, the state of the Siddha or perfected Master, in which one perceives the world and everything in it as the light of Shiva in various forms.

Sahasrāra: The thousand-petaled lotus at the crown of the head, the highest spiritual center in the human being, where the union of Shiva and Shakti takes place.

Samādhi: A state of meditative union with the Absolute.

Saṃskāras: Impressions left by thoughts or actions in the past, which form our mental and emotional conditioning. They are stored in the *suṣumnā*.

Saṅdhi: A transition from one thing to another.

Saṅdhyā: The morning and evening twilights.

Saṅkalpa: Thought or will, one of the four classical methods by which the Guru gives *śaktipāt*.

Sannyāsi: An ascetic ordained as a monk; a renunciant, who has taken the formal vows of renunciation.

Saraswati: The goddess of music, knowledge, fluency in speech, and creative inspiration.

Saundarya Laharī: "Wave of Beauty," one of the most inspiring of all the devotional poems to the *Devī*, composed by Shankaracharya. It includes a description of the physical beauty of the *Devī*'s form.

Self: Divine Consciousness residing in the individual.

Serpent Power, The: A work by Sir John Woodroffe, containing two texts on Kundalini, the *Ṣaṭ Chakra Nirūpaṇa* and the *Pādukā Pañchaka*, with a lengthy introduction and commentary.

Śabda Brahman: The Absolute in the form of sound; the divine inner *nāda*.

Shakti: Spiritual power; the divine cosmic power which creates and maintains the universe.

Śakti dāridrya: Poverty of Shakti; the condition of an individual soul whose powers have been limited and contracted by *māyā*.

Śaktipāt: The descent of grace; the transmission of Shakti or spiritual power from the Guru to the disciple.

Śambhavi mudrā: A state of spontaneous *samādhi* in which the eyes become focused within although they remain half-open.

Shankaracharya (788-820): A great sage who traveled throughout India expounding Advaita Vedanta, the philosophy of Absolute Nondualism, which teaches the identity of the individual soul and the supreme Soul. He established maths or ashrams in the four corners of India.

Śāradā Tilaka Tantra: A great work by Lakshmana Deshikendra, disciple of Utpalacharya. He is said to have written the work out of compassion for those who wanted to know something about all the different forms of worship. It also deals with yoga and Kundalini.

Ṣaṭ Chakra Nirūpaṇa: "An Investigation of the Six *Chakras*," a Sanskrit text composed in the sixteenth century by the great Master Purnananda Swami.

Shiva: The all-pervasive supreme Reality; one of the Hindu trinity of gods, who carries out the act of destruction or dissolution.

Śiva liṅgam: The most important symbol of Shiva, representing the impersonal aspect of God.

Śiva Mahimnaḥ Stotram: "Hymn to the Glory of Shiva," sung in the evening in Siddha Yoga Ashrams.

Śiva Saṁhitā: A Sanskrit text on yoga which explains the practice of *āsanas*, *prāṇāyāma*, and *mudrās*, performed in order to awaken Kundalini.

Śiva Stotrāvalī Ṭīkā: Kshemaraja's commentary on the *Śiva Stotrāvalī*, a collection of verses to Shiva by Utpaladeva; a devotional work belonging to the tradition of Kashmir Shaivism.

Śiva Sūtras: A Sanskrit text which Lord Shiva revealed to the sage Vasugupta. It consists of seventy-seven *sūtras*, or aphorisms, which were found inscribed on a rock in Kashmir.

Śiva Sūtra Vimarśinī: A commentary on the *Śiva Sūtras* by Kshemaraja.

Siddha: A perfected Master; one who has attained the state of unity-awareness and who experiences himself as all-pervasive.

Siddhis: Supernatural powers attained through mantra repetition, meditation, and other yogic practices.

South Fallsburg, New York: The location of Shree Muktananda

Ashram, established as the international headquarters of the SYDA Foundation in 1979.

Spanda Śāstras: A body of philosophical works in Kashmir Shaivism which elaborate the principles of the *Śiva Sūtras*. The main text is the *Spanda Kārikās*, on which a number of commentaries have been written: the *Spanda Pradīpikā* by Utpalabhatta, the *Spandakārikā Vivritti* by Ramakantha, and the *Spanda Sandoha* and the *Spanda Nirṇaya* by Kshemaraja.

Sriṣṭi-krama: The process of creation; the return of Kundalini from the *sahasrāra* to the *mūlādhāra chakra*.

Subtle body: An energy body interpenetrating the physical body; according to the *Prāśna Upaniṣad*, the subtle body is composed of 720 million *nāḍīs*. It is the body in which we experience the dream state, and its seat is in the throat. It is associated with a thumb-sized white light.

Supracausal body: The body in which we experience the *turīya*, or transcendental state. It is a scintillating blue dot the size of a lentil seed and is called the *bindu* or Blue Pearl. Its seat is the *sahasrāra*.

Suṣumnā: The most important of all the *nāḍīs*, the central channel which extends from the base of the spine to the crown of the head. It is the pathway of the awakened Kundalini.

Svacchanda Tantra: A revealed scripture in six volumes in the tradition of Kashmir Shaivism, dealing with rituals and yogic techniques.

Svādhiṣṭhāna chakra: The energy center within the *suṣumnā* in the sacral area.

Svāhā: "Hail to!" An exclamation used in making offerings to the deities during a *yajña*, a sacred fire ceremony.

Swami or Swamiji: A term of respectful address for a *sannyāsi*, or monk.

Tantrāloka: A massive and encyclopedic work by Abhinavagupta in twelve volumes, containing the Shaiva philosophy and practices in all their aspects.

Tantras: Divinely revealed scriptures in the form of dialogues between Shiva and Parvati, revealing the secrets of attaining Self-realization through Kundalini awakening and through uniting the two principles, Shiva and Shakti.

Tantrasāra: A summary of the teachings of the *Tantrāloka* by Abhinavagupta.

Tattva: A principle of creation; according to Kashmir Shaivism, there are thirty-six *tattvas* from Shiva to the earth.

Tirumular: A South Indian saint who lived around the eighth century.

Tīvra: The intense degree of *śaktipāt*.

Triveṇi: The place of confluence of the three sacred rivers: Ganga, Yamuna, and Saraswati, represented in the human body by the *īḍā*, *piṅgalā*, and *suṣumnā nāḍīs*. *Yukta-triveṇi* is at the *mūlādhāra chakra*, and *mukta-triveṇi* is at the *ājñā chakra*.

Tukaram Maharaj (1608-1650): A great poet-saint of Maharashtra born at Dehu, who composed thousands of *abhangas*, devotional songs in Marathi.

Turīya: The fourth or transcendental state of consciousness beyond the states of waking, dreaming, and deep sleep, and pervading all the states; the state of the Self.

Uma: A name for Shakti, meaning light. This aspect represents the power to illuminate, or pure knowledge.

Ūnmanī: The Shakti which transcends the mind and is uninterrupted light.

Upaniṣads: The teachings of the ancient sages that form the knowledge or the end portion of the Vedas. The central teaching of the *Upaniṣads* is that the Self of man is the same as the Absolute.

Vajra: A subtle, sunlike *nāḍī* within the *suṣumnā*.

Varṇamayī: One of the four main categories of the manifestation of awakened Kundalini. This may include the awakening of previously dormant vocal powers in a seeker, the spontaneous uttering of mantras or other sounds, creative literary inspiration, and intuitive wisdom. *Varṇamayī* pertains to *mantra yoga*.

Vāyavīya Saṁhitā: The concluding section of the *Śiva Purāṇa*.

Vedānta: One of the schools of Indian philosophy. It contains the teachings of the *Upaniṣads*, which investigate the nature and relationship of the Absolute, the world, and the Self.

Vedas: The four ancient, authoritative Hindu scriptures, regarded as divinely revealed. The four *Vedas* are the *Rig Veda*, *Yajur Veda*, *Sama Veda*, and *Atharva Veda*.

Vedhamayī: One of the four main categories of the manifestation of awakened Kundalini, in which a seeker experiences the piercing of the *chakras*. *Vedhamayī* is associated with *laya yoga*.

Videha kaivalya: The final absorption into Consciousness of a realized being when he leaves his physical body; bodiless liberation.

Vidyā: One of the five *kañchukas*. It restricts the universal power of omniscience and is the cause of limited knowledge.

Vijñāna Bhairava: A revealed text of Kashmir Shaivism, containing one hundred twelve *dhāraṇās* or centering techniques for entering into Shiva.

Visarga: Emanation, creation.

Vishnu: A name for the all-pervasive supreme Reality; one of the Hindu trinity of gods, representing God as the sustainer.

Viśuddha chakra: The energy center at the base of the throat.

Viveka Chūḍāmaṇi: "The Crest-Jewel of Discrimination," Shankaracharya's classic text of Advaita Vedanta.

Vritti: A mental or emotional quality associated with a particular *chakra*.

Vyāpti: Fusion, the process in which the gross *tattvas* are reabsorbed into the subtler ones. *Ātma-vyāpti* is merging with the inner Self. *Śiva-vyāpti* is merging with the all-pervasive Shiva principle; the realization that the whole world is an aspect of the Self.

Wish-fulfilling cow: The sacred cow, considered to be a goddess who has the power to give milk whenever needed by gods and sages, and who grants one's wishes.

Wish-fulfilling tree: A celestial tree that has the power to grant the wish of anyone standing under it.

Yatra: Pilgrimage.

Yoga: The state of union with the Self, God; the practices leading to that state.

Yoga braṣṭha: One who practiced yoga but was unable to complete his *sādhana* in a former lifetime. He continues his spiritual practice at the level of attainment he achieved and attains perfection in a later birth.

Yogakuṇḍalī Upaniṣad: A *Yoga Upaniṣad* of the *Kriṣṇa Yajur Veda*, dealing with the awakening and rising of Kundalini.

INDEX

Abhinavagupta
  on types of *śaktipāt*, 46-50

Air
  and *anāhata chakra*, 98-99

Ājñā chakra, 23, 105-8, 120
  and Blue Pearl, 108
  deity of, 106
  liṅgam in, 106
  and mind, 105-6
  nāda (divine sounds) at, 111
  and *prakriti*, 105-6
  and the *sahasrāra*, 111
  as seat of Guru, 105
  seed mantra of, 85, 105, 107
  Shakti of, 106

A-ka-tha triangle, 113-15

Anāhata (heart) *chakra*, 24, 97-102
  and air, 98-99
  deity of, 99
  and *Haṁsah*, 98
  liṅgam in, 99
  nāda (divine sounds) in, 78
  piercing of, 76
  qualities of, 99
  seat of deity in, 99-100
  seed mantra of, 85-98
  Shakti of, 99

Bandhas, 61. See also *haṭha yoga*

Bīja mantras (seed letters), 84

Blue Pearl
  in *sahasrāra*, 115-16

Body
  causal, 25
  gross physical, 25
  subtle, 25
  supracausal, 24

Brahma, 114
  as deity of *mūlādhāra chakra*, 86, 89

Buddhism, 10-11

Causal body, 25, 111

Chakras
  and association with sounds, 69-70
  deities of, 83, 85-86
  as energy centers, 82-83
  liṅgams in, 87
  as lotuses, 83
  lower vs. higher, 73, 74, 94
  and material elements, 84
  "petals" of, 83
  piercing of, 75-78
  seed letters of, 84
  and the senses, 85
  Shaktis of, 86
  and *tattvas*, 82
  See also *ājñā chakra*; *anāhata chakra*; *maṇipūra chakra*; *mūlādhāra chakra*; *sahasrāra*; Subtle body; *svādhiṣṭhāna chakra*; *viśuddha chakra*

Chidvilasananda, Swami
  on the *ājñā chakra*, 106
  on the Blue Pearl, 115
  on the goal of meditation, 112
  on the Goddess, 20
  on Kundalini, 91, 92, 94
  on the *viśuddha chakra*, 104

Cloaks (*kañchukas*), 26-27

Depression, 60

Dīkṣā. See *śaktipāt*

Earth
  and *mūlādhāra chakra*, 88-89

Ether
and *viśuddha chakra*, 102-3

Fire, 87-88, 114
and *maṇipūra chakra*, 93-97

Grace, 32-34
as divine function, 32
See also Guru

Great Void (*mahā śūnya*), 115-16

Gross physical body, 25

Guru
as bestower of initiation (*śaktipāt*), 33-42
as controller of awakened Kundalini, 41-42, 92-93
as grace-bestowing power of God, 33

Gurumayi
See Chidvilasananda, Swami

Haṁsah, 98

Haṭha yoga, 31-32
bandhas (locks) in, 63
and *kriyās* after *śaktipāt*, 62-69
mudrās in, 63-65
origin of, 62
prāṇāyāma in, 65-68

Hearing, 102-3, 119

Heart *chakra*. See *anāhata chakra*

Heart opening, 76
See also *anāhata chakra*

Hopi Indians, 5-6

Īḍā nāḍī, 87-88
See also *nāḍīs*

Initiation, See *śaktipāt*

Involution, 23, 26

Isha
as deity of *anāhata chakra*, 86, 99

Kabbala, 7-8

Kabir
poems of, 4, 81

Kalāvati (*śaktipāt* manifestation), 73-75

Kali
as form of Shakti, 19

Kañchukas (cloaks), 26-27

Kriyās
as beneficial, 57, 67-68
emotional, 56-57
after *śaktipāt* (in *kriyāvati*), 62-69
witnessing of, 57
See also *haṭha yoga*

Kriyāvati (*śaktipāt* manifestation), 62-69

Kundalini
in Christianity, 4-5
as the Great Goddess, 15-20
in Jewish mysticism, 7-8
means of awakening, 31-42
names for, 3
in other cultures, 3-13
path of, 119-20
seen as serpent, 8-10
See also Kundalini yoga, *śaktipāt*

Kundalini yoga, 92-93

Kung of the Kalahari Desert, 6-7

Lakshmi
as form of Shakti, 19-20

Laya (absorption, merging), 119, 120

Letters
of Sanskrit, 83

Liberation, 125-26

Locks, 61
See also *bandhas*

Lotuses. See *chakras*

Macrocosm
identity with microcosm, 81

Mahā śūnya. See Great Void

Maṇipūra (navel) *chakra*, 24, 93-97
deity of, 94
and fire, 93-97
qualities of, 94
seed mantra of, 85, 93
Shakti of, 94

Index

Swami Muktananda

SIDDHA YOGA

and the Lineage of Siddha Masters

Siddha Yoga begins with the awakening of the transformative power known in the Indian tradition as Kundalini. This path to union with the Divine is guided by the grace of a living Master, a Siddha. In the ancient tradition of the Siddhas, through the Guru's graceful glance or sacred word of initiation, this inner power is kindled and the student is awakened into a more subtle awareness. As Kundalini unfolds, all the limiting, negative qualities dissolve, and divine virtues arise — love, compassion, generosity, wisdom. Thus, the awakening, joined with the disciplines of yoga, leads to the attainment of higher knowledge and, ultimately, to Self-realization or enlightenment.

The capacity to awaken Kundalini has always been rare. In our own century, the Siddha Master Swami Muktananda initiated this process in thousands of seekers. He had himself received spiritual initiation, known as *śaktipāt* ("descent of power"), from the great soul Bhagawan Nityananda, who was then living in the village of Ganeshpuri in west central India. On August 15, 1947, a day that Muktananda later described as "the happiest and most auspicious day of my life," Nityananda stood close to his disciple, and a ray of golden light began to pour out of his eyes and into Muktananda's. Kundalini Shakti, which stirred within Muktananda in that moment, bestowed Her amazing fruits upon him even as he walked home from his Guru's

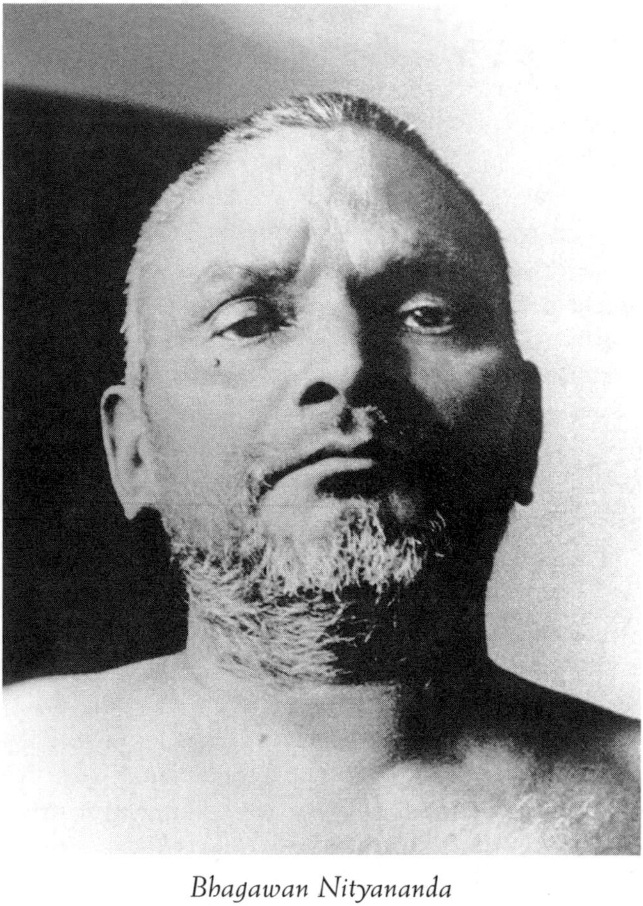

Bhagawan Nityananda

darśan hall. On that quiet country road, in the drifting mists of a monsoon shower, Muktananda had the experience of the Absolute, of God-consciousness pervading every particle of the phenomenal world.

Swami Muktananda meditated in seclusion for nine years, seeing fewer and fewer people, simplifying every aspect of his life, increasing the focus of his spiritual practice, as with the laser beam of devotion and intention he penetrated layer after layer of ignorance and illusion. Ultimately he had the vision of his Guru, Nityananda; of his deity, Lord Shiva; and of his own form within a scintillating blue light, which then shattered to spread throughout the universe. This vision, of the oneness and the divinity of all things, stayed with Swami Muktananda to the end of his life.

Bhagawan Nityananda settled his disciple on a small piece of land near his own ashram in Ganeshpuri, and here Muktananda stayed, receiving visitors sent by his Guru and performing devotional practices. At the time of Bhagawan Nityananda's death in 1961, Muktananda received a further level of initiation in which the power of Nityananda's lineage to give *śaktipāt* was transferred to him.

Swami Muktananda spent the remainder of his life giving *śaktipāt* and writing and speaking about the path of meditation that begins with this awakening. His ashram, which is now known as Gurudev Siddha Peeth, flourished as a center of spiritual power and instruction, as seekers of every creed and from every country were welcomed by Muktananda's vision of the divinity residing within the heart of every human being.

This great work has been expanded by his foremost disciple, Swami Chidvilasananda, who was designated by Swami Muktananda as his successor shortly before

Swami Chidvilasananda

his death in 1982. She had been his disciple since early childhood and had traveled with him on two tours of the West, translating into English his writings, his lectures, and the many informal exchanges he had with his devotees. An advanced spiritual seeker from an early age, with a great longing for God, she became an exemplary disciple. She was guided meticulously in her *sādhana* by Swami Muktananda, who carefully prepared her to succeed him as Guru. In early May of 1982, Swami Chidvilasananda took formal vows of monkhood, and a few days later, Swami Muktananda bequeathed to her the power and authority of the Siddha lineage, the same spiritual legacy that his Guru had passed on to him. Since that time, Gurumayi, as she is widely known, has given *śaktipāt* to ever-increasing numbers of seekers, awakening in them the divine power that is worshiped by Siddhas as the Goddess. In the words of Swami Muktananda:

> Kundalini is Shakti, supreme energy, whom the sages worship as the Mother of the universe. Yogis make Her the goal of their yoga. Devotees sing Her name with love, and She becomes the object of their love. Enlightened men of knowledge perceive Her in all the forms and objects of the universe, and seeing everything as one in That, they merge in That.

FURTHER READING

Swami Muktananda

Play of Consciousness
From the Finite to the Infinite
Where Are You Going?
I Have Become Alive
The Perfect Relationship
Reflections of the Self
Secret of the Siddhas
I Am That
Kundalini
Mystery of the Mind
Does Death Really Exist?
Light on the Path
In the Company of a Siddha
Lalleshwari
Mukteshwari
Meditate

Swami Chidvilasananda

My Lord Loves a Pure Heart
Kindle My Heart
Ashes at My Guru's Feet

You may learn more about the
teachings and practices of
Siddha Yoga Meditation by contacting:

SYDA Foundation
P.O. Box 600,
371 Brickman Rd.
South Fallsburg, NY 12779-0600, USA
Tel: (914) 434-2000

or

Gurudev Siddha Peeth
PIN 401 206
P.O. Ganeshpuri
District Thana
Maharashtra, India

For further information about books in print
by Swami Muktananda
and Swami Chidvilasananda,
and editions in translation, please contact:

Siddha Yoga Meditation Bookstore
P.O. Box 600,
371 Brickman Rd.
South Fallsburg, NY 12779-0600, USA
Tel: (914) 434-2000 ext. 1700

Call toll-free from the United States and Canada: 888 422-3334
Fax toll-free from the United States and Canada: 888 422-3339